The **BOOK** *of* UNEXPLAINED MYSTERIES

The **BOOK** of **UNEXPLAINED MYSTERIES**

On the Trail of the Secret and the Strange

WILL PEARSON

WEIDENFELD & NICOLSON

First published in Great Britain in 2019 by Weidenfeld & Nicolson
an imprint of The Orion Publishing Group Ltd
Carmelite House, 50 Victoria Embankment
London EC4Y 0DZ

An Hachette UK Company

1 3 5 7 9 10 8 6 4 2

A CIP catalogue record for this book is
available from the British Library.

ISBN HB 9781474609500

ISBN eBook 9781474609524

Typeset by Input Data Services Ltd, Somerset

Printed and bound in Great Britain by Clays Ltd, Elcograf S.p.A.

www.weidenfeldandnicolson.co.uk

This book is dedicated to Gaynor Aaltonen,
who made it better.

Acknowledgements

Thanks to Alan Samson, whose idea this all was in the first place; to Simon English, who burnished more than just the tautologies; to Tom Voigt of zodiackiller.com for his invaluable help; and to Forrest Fenn, for kind permission to include his treasure hunt.

Contents

Introduction

Everybody loves a good mystery, be it a crime novel, the strange behaviour of the universe, or some of the odd goings-on in the animal kingdom. Is 'the answer to the ultimate question of life, the universe and everything' really '42', as Douglas Adams playfully suggests in *The Hitchhiker's Guide to the Galaxy*? Probably not – although scientists working on the Large Hadron Collider in CERN may know something we don't: they recently dubbed their new office complex 'Building 42'.

Sometimes, the questions can be more interesting than the answers. The Search for Extraterrestrial Intelligence (SETI) has recently hotted up, with a whole new wave of research going to show that we will always be fascinated by what we don't understand. Was the Wow! Signal a radio transmission from deep space? Or was it the ambient resonating frequency of a passing comet?

Occasionally, it can feel as if there's a conspiracy at work – one in which scientists, journalists and professional explainers of all stripes want to put an end to anything and everything mysterious in life. It's a bit disappointing, for example, to be told that sea-level changes caused by the last Ice Age mitigate against the probability of plesiosaurs surviving in Loch Ness. This might help explain the ever-increasing popularity of fantasy films, novels, video games, and stories brought to us in virtual reality.

Thankfully, not everything in life can be pegged out, nailed down, sucked dry of its secrets and turned into a factoid. Mysteries do still exist – and unsolved mysteries – to burnish a tautology – continue to tease us.

The twenty mysteries we look at in this book explore a broad spectrum of strangeness. Each in its own unique way presents a challenge. Some, like the sudden disappearance of the sailing ship *Mary Celeste*'s passengers and crew have gained universal currency. Others, like the Wow! Signal, are much more recent and perhaps a bit less well known. Cryptids like Bigfoot and the Loch Ness Monster teeter on the boundaries of probable and improbable, hoax and reality, fact and fiction. Sceptic or believer, the fun lies in probing them.

The Shugborough Code

What is the meaning of the Shugborough Code, the ten-letter inscription carved into the base of a sculpture at Shugborough Hall, in Staffordshire, England? For more than 250 years, the mystery has remained unsolved. In order to help explain it, we need to go back to one of the greatest and most daring voyages in British naval history . . .

Rain lashed HMS *Centurion*, reducing visibility to less than a mile. Then, as quickly as it had pounced, the squall lifted. High in the crow's nest, the lookout wiped his eyes. He had glimpsed something through a gap in the grey curtain. Or had he? He stared at the horizon, waiting for the man-o'-war to overtop the seething, grey-green shoulder of the next wave. As it lifted and then hung for a moment, he raised the glass to his eye for a second look. There was no mistake. Smack on the horizon, the intermittent flash of a sail. A topgallant, stretched tight to catch the strengthening wind. Cupping his hands, the lookout leaned and shouted, 'Ship ahoy! Fine on the starboard bow!'

On the quarterdeck, Commodore George Anson felt a great surge of relief. And resolve. He had gambled everything on this moment: his career, his reputation, and his personal fortune. Let it not be some sluggish merchantman, with nothing but foodstuffs in her hold. Let this be the prize he'd been seeking for these many months. With no outward show of the excitement he felt within, Anson gave the order to make all sail. On her present course, the stranger was heading away from the *Centurion*. His task was to overhaul her. And fight.

Things had not started well for Anson's squadron. It was made up of six men-o'-war: the flagship, HMS *Centurion*, a fourth-rate of 1,005 tons, 400 men and 60 guns; His Majesty's Ships *Gloucester* and *Severn*, both 853 tons, 300 men and 50 guns; HMS *Pearl*, 600 tons, 250 men and 40 guns; HMS *Wager*, 599 tons, 120 men and 24 guns; and the nimble little sloop *Tryal*, 200 tons, 70 men and 8 guns. Two merchant vessels, the *Anna* and the *Industry* ferried supplies.

The flotilla weighed anchor from St Helen's, off the Isle of Wight, on 18 September 1740, and set sail into a contrary wind. Anson's orders were to capture and ransack one of the Spanish treasure ships that crossed the Pacific annually from Acapulco. Their Lordships of the British Admiralty also wanted the squadron to take the port of Callao and the Peruvian capital Lima by force; incite and lead a popular Peruvian revolution to overthrow Spanish rule; capture Panama with all of its treasure; and 'use [his] best endeavours to annoy and distress the Spaniards, either at sea or land . . . by sinking, burning or otherwise destroying all their ships and vessels you shall meet with.' In his spare time, the Commodore was also to capture Manila.

Their Lords of the Admiralty were very good at making demands. They were very bad when it came to helping Anson meet them. The 500 troops they'd assigned the squadron were far too few for purpose. Even worse, instead of sending him strong, fit and well-trained men, the powers-that-be ordered Anson to collect 500 invalids from the Chelsea Hospital. On hearing that they were to be forced back to sea, many of the invalids absconded. In the event, only 259 reported for duty in Portsmouth harbour; many were already in their sixties and seventies. Some of them were so old and infirm they had to be carried aboard on stretchers. Anson tried to send them back. The Admiralty ordered him to take them. In order to make up the missing numbers, some 210 Marines were told to join the squadron. It sounded good, but in almost every case these additional men were red raw recruits, who had not even been taught how to shoot. It was a bad beginning – and it seemed to lay a curse on the expedition.

By the time it reached St Catherine's (modern Ilha de Santa Catarina) in southern Brazil, roughly half the squadron's men were either dead of the scarlet fever, or the next thing to it. Typhus, brought on by the chronic overcrowding below decks, also took its toll. More men were suffering the horrors of scurvy: extreme lassitude, swollen and bleeding gums, foul breath and teeth that were loose where they had not fallen out – and a lingering death.

Anson let the crew recuperate on dry land, buying fresh fruit and vegetables to speed their recovery. By now, he was a long way behind the proposed schedule. Unless he got a move on, the enemy treasure galleon would be gone by the time he reached the Philippines. The penalty? He would be forced to round Cape Horn in winter – at the very worst and most dangerous time of year.

The ferocious gales around Cape Horn at that time of year were known to strip ships of their rigging, sails and masts. Great seas whipped up by the wind towered high and then smashed down on anything and everything in their path, carrying men and material away in a trice. Crews had a saying: below forty degrees south there is no law. Below fifty, there is no God. The Cape lies at 55.98 degrees south.

Three months later, all eight ships were still battling to round the Cape. Crunched in the jaws of ferocious storms, the squadron tacked and turned repeatedly, determined to batter its way west. Exhausted and freezing, more men died of exposure. Frostbite stalked the remainder, taking fingers and toes. Scarlet fever once again set about its lethal work: 45 men died in April, with a further 80 succumbing in May. By the middle of June 1741, Anson had lost more than 200 of his command. Even today, it counts as one of the most arduous – and some would say horrific – journeys in the annals of seafaring.

With barely enough men to work ship, the *Centurion* finally made it to Socorro on the coast of Chile. By now, the flagship was alone. Any grandiose plans to take Callao, or lead a popular revolution against Peru's colonial government were out of the question. When none of the other ships had reached the agreed rendezvous a fortnight later, the *Centurion* sailed on to the island of Juan Fernández. Here, personally helping to carry some of the sickest men ashore, Anson once again tried to nurse his crew back to health. HMS *Gloucester* and HMS *Tryal* arrived at the island a fortnight later. They brought little comfort. If anything, their crews were even more ravaged by death and disease than the *Centurion*'s. The Commodore ordered a head count: of the 961 men who had set sail with him, only 351 were left alive – many of them boys. Later, he would learn that the *Severn* and the *Pearl* had entirely abandoned the attempt to round the Horn and sailed back to Brazil. HMS *Wager* had been driven ashore and wrecked. The survivors, among them the poet Byron's grandfather, were stranded and starving on a barren stretch of coast. This led to mutiny and further disaster, with no more than a handful of the *Wager*'s crew surviving to tell the tale.

Despite all these setbacks, and with exemplary devotion to duty, Anson set about harassing the Spanish and their possessions as best he could. Over the next few weeks, his three-ship command succeeded in capturing several valuable Spanish merchantmen, including *La Nuestra del Monte Carmel*. Scuttling

HMS *Tryal*, which had suffered terminal damage rounding the Cape, Anson replaced her with one of the prizes.

With this initial success having helped raise morale, Anson next led a tiny band of men in a surprise raid on the wealthy Spanish-held town of Payta. Nestled in a bay on the coast of Chile, it was a known source of silver. With muffled oars, the 58 British raiders stole ashore in the very dead of night. Screeching and shouting, banging drums and firing off their muskets, they raised several incarnations of hell. Terrified by the din, and with memories of the ruthless English pirate Drake to spur them on, Payta's 10,000 citizens ran for the hills. Clad only in their nightclothes, they were convinced that a much larger force was attacking them. Anson's ruse had paid off.

When Payta's governor proudly – and unwisely – refused Anson's offer of parley, the Commodore ordered his men to pillage and then set fire to the town. They needed no second bidding. Stripping off their own filthy rags, they fell upon the finery the *Paytanos* had left behind. Some of the men were so excited, they pulled silk gowns and other female wear on over the breeches and jackets they'd already donned. From the Payta Customs House alone they stole pieces of eight (Spanish silver dollars) and plate to the value of some £30,000. It was a partial return for all the hardships they had suffered – but for Anson, it wasn't enough.

A few days later, the *Centurion* took a further £12,000 in booty from another Spanish merchant ship unlucky enough to cross its track. Despite its puny strength, Anson's squadron was fulfilling his secondary mission – to harass and annoy the Spanish crown wherever possible.

In February 1742, the *Centurion* and the *Gloucester* headed for Acapulco. Anson wanted to see if any of the treasure galleons were still in port, or had already left. Three captured Spanish fishermen told him that one galleon had arrived there three weeks earlier. A second, bound for Manila, was due to sail in two weeks' time. With so few men left at his command, Anson decided to cut his losses and head for home. The sensible route now lay west across the Pacific via Macao, and if possible, Canton. The two ships had barely cleared land when ill-luck and bad weather struck again: the *Gloucester* lost its mainmast and sprang an unstoppable leak. More men were dying on both ships. Anson ordered the stricken *Gloucester* to be cleared of anything useful and set ablaze. What was left of her crew transferred to the *Centurion* and they battled on.

On 21 October 1742 the flagship reached Canton (now Guangzhou), China – the first British warship ever to make port there. Used to harmless merchantmen, the Chinese did not in any way take kindly to the presence of a foreign warship and its scurvy-looking crew. At anchor in the roads, Anson had the devil's own work persuading the city's Mandarins to let him repair, resupply and refit his ship. At last, and with a great deal of reluctance, the Chinese allowed him to dock. A certain elegant hint of bombardment is rumoured to have encouraged the change of heart. Once the much-needed repairs had been completed, Anson settled his bills and set sail. In place of his original British crew, he now had seamen of every creed and colour, all of them paid and persuaded to join in Macao. In total, he had scraped up 227 men – barely more than half the flagship's normal complement of 400.

Rather than return to England with nothing to show for the expedition but dead men, lost ships and eighty pieces of silver, Anson decided to risk everything on one last gamble. If *Centurion* now made for Manila, it was just possible she might, even now, run across one of the Spanish treasure ships. The danger was that if both the great Acapulco galleons he knew to have been in port there caught him at the same time, the *Centurion* was finished.

A few weeks later, the flagship reached Cape Espiritu Santo, on the north-eastern tip of Samar Island, in the Philippines. The waters here lay directly on the preferred Spanish route to Manila. The *Centurion* set to patrolling. Days and weeks went by, with no sign of the fabled treasure ships. Anson used the time to drill his new recruits on the guns, loading, running out and firing repeatedly until they were quick and assured. He also set the best shots among the Marines to extra marksmanship practice. If they did cross an enemy ship, their job was to man the mast tops and use their muskets to pick off its officers. As the days turned into weeks, the wait became debilitating – but Anson was nothing if not dogged. He knew that if he returned home empty-handed, his career – and his reputation – were at stake.

On 20 June 1743, Anson's luck turned. Spanish spies had learned of his mission even before he left England. Hoping to outwit him, they had delayed the departure of the latest treasure shipment by several weeks. The ploy played right into the Commodore's hands. All the setbacks the squadron had suffered meant that now, the *Centurion* was in the right place at the right time.

The Ambush

The weather cleared, and the flagship slowly began to overhaul the fleeing vessel. As its lines resolved from the haze, the spirits of every man on board the *Centurion* soared. It was a great, fat-bellied Spanish galleon, groaning with treasure – the prize they had suffered every kind of hell to attain. The weight of her precious cargo meant that *La Nuestra Señora de Covadonga*, as the vessel turned out to be, was sitting deep in the water. That extra draught was slowing her down. The only thing now between the British and a fortune in Spanish silver was the *Covadonga*'s guns, and the fighting spirit of her 550-strong crew. Boasting 22 eighteen-pounder cannon; 22 twelve-pounders; 6 eight-pounders; and 24 '*pedreroes*', or swivel-guns that were deadly at short range, the galleon outgunned the *Centurion* by some chalk. No matter. Anson ordered 'hands to quarters'. *Centurion* cleared for action and ran out her own guns. The yeoman of signals broke out the broad red British battle ensign, and hoisted the Commodore's pennant.

It might be bloody, it might prove costly, and it might prove long, but the Battle for the Spanish Treasure was on.

The Battle for the Covadonga

The (abridged) diary of Richard Walter, the *Centurion*'s chaplain, titled *Lord Anson's Voyage Round the World* (1749), tells us what happened next:

> The Commodore picked out about thirty of his choicest hands and best marksmen, whom he distributed into his tops, and who fully answered his expectation by the signal services they performed. As he had not hands enough remaining to quarter a sufficient number to each great gun, he therefore fixed only 2 men to each gun, who were to be solely employed in loading it.
>
> The rest of his people he divided into different gangs of ten or 12 men each. They continually moved about the decks, to run out and fire such guns as were loaded. By this management he was enabled to make use of all his guns; and instead of whole broadsides, with intervals between them, he kept up a constant fire without intermission; whence he doubted not to procure very signal advantages. For it is common with the Spaniards to fall down upon the decks when they see a broadside preparing,

and continue in that posture till it is given; after which they rise again, and presuming the danger to be for some time over, work their own guns and fire with great briskness, till another enemy broadside is ready. But the firing of gun by gun, in the manner directed by the Commodore, rendered this practice of theirs impossible.

. . . Towards one o'clock, the *Centurion* came within gunshot of the galleon. The Commodore perceiving the Spaniards to have neglected clearing their ship till that time, as he saw them throwing overboard cattle and lumber, he gave orders to fire upon them with the chase-guns. This was to disturb them in their work, and prevent them from completing it. The galleon returned fire with two of her stern chasers . . . The *Centurion* rigged her sprit-sail-yard fore and aft, so as to be ready for boarding. The Spaniards, in Bravado, rigged their own sprit-sail-yard fore and aft likewise.

Soon after, the *Centurion* came abreast of the enemy. We were now within pistol shot. We kept to leeward of them, to prevent their putting before the wind and gaining the port of Jalapay, from which they were about 7 leagues distant.

The engagement now began in earnest. For the first half hour, Mr. Anson over-reached the galleon, and lay on her bow, where by the great wideness of his ports he could traverse almost all his guns upon the enemy, whilst the galleon could only bring some of hers to bear. As soon as the action began, the mats with which the galleon had stuffed her netting took fire and burnt violently, blazing up half as high as the mizzen top. This accident, caused by the *Centurion*'s cannon wads, threw the enemy into the utmost terror. It also alarmed the Commodore – he feared lest the galleon should be burned, and the *Centurion* with her. However the Spaniards at last freed themselves from the fire by cutting away the netting, tumbling the whole flaming mass into the sea.

All this interval the *Centurion* kept her first advantageous position, firing her cannon with great regularity and briskness. At the same time the galleon's decks lay open to our top-men. Having at their first volley driven the Spaniards from their tops, they made prodigious havoc with their small arms, killing or wounding every officer but one that appeared on the quarter-deck, and wounding in particular the General of the galleon himself.

Thus the action proceeded for at least half an hour. But then the *Centurion* lost the superiority arising from her original situation, and was close alongside the galleon. The enemy continued to fire briskly for near an hour longer; yet even in this posture the Commodore's grapeshot swept their decks so effectually, and the number of their slain and wounded became so considerable, that they began to fall into great disorder, especially as the General, who was the life of the action, was no longer capable of exerting himself.

Their confusion was visible from onboard the *Centurion*; for the ships were so near that some of the Spanish officers were seen running about with much assiduity to prevent the desertion of their men from their quarters. But all their endeavours were in vain; for after having, as a last effort, fired five or six guns with more judgment than usual, they yielded up the contest. The galleon's colours being already singed off the ensign staff, she struck the standard flying at her main topgallant masthead.

Thus was the *Centurion* possessed of this rich prize, amounting in value to near a million-and-a-half of dollars. She was called the *Nostra Signora de Cobadonga* [*sic*], and was commanded by General Don Jeronimo de Montero, a Portuguese, who was the most approved officer for skill and courage of any employed in that service. The galleon was much larger than the *Centurion*, and had five hundred and fifty men and thirty-six guns mounted for action, besides twenty-eight pedreroes in her gunwale, quarters and tops, each of which carried a four-pound ball . . . She had sixty-seven men killed in the action, and eighty-four wounded, whilst the *Centurion* had only two killed, and a lieutenant and sixteen wounded, all of whom but one recovered.

The treasure thus taken by the *Centurion* having been, for at least eighteen months, the great object of their hopes, it was impossible to describe the transport on board, when, after all their reiterated disappointments, they at last saw their wishes accomplished.

The Commodore resolved to make the best of his way with his prize for the river of Canton . . . Securing the prisoners was a matter of still more consequence, as not only the possession of the treasure, but the lives of the captors depended thereon. This gave the Commodore much trouble and disquietude, for they were above double the number of his own people. Some of them when they were brought on board the *Centurion*, and had observed how slenderly she was manned . . . could not help expressing themselves with great indignation, to be thus beaten by a handful of boys.

A separate account of the voyage tells us that, in an effort to stop the British getting their hands on it, the *Covadonga*'s crew had hidden the bulk of her phenomenal treasure as ingeniously as they could:

Aboard the *Covadonga*, Saumarez was continually finding more treasure hidden in false ceilings and secreted behind panels. On one occasion, a suspiciously heavy load of cheeses that were sliced open was found to contain solid gold bullion. To date [July 1743] 1,278,546 Spanish gold and silver dollars and thousands of pounds in weight of beautifully wrought silver and gold have been discovered. In addition, the *Centurion* carried the treasure of Payta and other Spanish prizes, which altogether amounted to over £500,000 in 1743. This excluded jewels and thousands of gold, silver and jade ornaments as well as tapestries, damasks and rare spices. [Leo Heaps, *Log of the Centurion*, 1973.]

Commodore Anson arrived home at Spithead on 15 June 1744, to a hero's welcome. The general ecstasy he met with was understandable: not only had he bloodied the King of Spain's nose, he had wrested more than £50 million in today's money from the Spanish exchequer. With a formidable armed escort to keep it safe, thirty-four horse-drawn carts hauled the plunder from Portsmouth to the Tower of London. Cheering crowds lined the route. Only the second English skipper to circumnavigate the globe since Sir Francis Drake, Anson was a national hero.

But his success had been won at a heavy price. Scarlet fever, typhus and 'the plague of the sea', scurvy, had killed hundreds of his men. Promoted Rear Admiral and awarded three-eighths of the prize money, Anson's reputation was now assured. So, too, was his personal fortune: at current values, his share came to more than £18 million. Even the 14-year-old powder monkeys got twenty years' pay apiece. Poor children who had often been forced into service, they would go home as local heroes, and make the fortunes of their happy families.

Where is the mystery in this, and what does it have to do with the Shugborough Code? To try and answer this, we need to look at the history of Shugborough Hall, then a modest manor house near Litchfield, Staffordshire. The property of George Anson's elder brother, Thomas, it was about to undergo an almighty transformation.

The Shugborough Code

A man in sudden possession of a large fortune needs the best help he can come by in spending it. And Admiral George Anson was now one of the richest men of his day. He had joined the Navy at the age of 12 and knew a great deal about the sea, fighting ships, and commanding men. But what did he know of culture, philosophy, or art? Perhaps not so much. But now that he was fabulously wealthy, George, with the help of his brother, Thomas, set about correcting this.

The Member of Parliament for nearby Litchfield, Thomas Anson, had long wanted to improve the plain, three-storeyed property which had been built in 1693 by his father, William. He felt that Shugborough's extensive grounds, too, provided scope for the kind of bold statement a modern British Enlightenment man could make.

A veteran of the Grand Tour, Thomas Anson loved his classical antiquity. Eager to reinvent himself as a kind of Graeco-Roman nobleman and with a fortune in Spanish gold and silver to spend, he set about turning Shugborough into a kind of vast neoclassical theme park. Once finished, he had no doubt it would transform himself, his heroic brother George and the rest of his family into standard bearers of the Enlightenment, that tidal wave of rational thinking, scientific enquiry and newly informed artistic taste that had seized the age.

With the money to employ some of the finest architects, designers, artists and sculptors of the period, Anson commissioned architect, astronomer and garden designer Thomas Wright of Durham to improve and enlarge the original seventeenth-century house, renew its interior, and sculpt out a new landscape.

He also employed the brilliant architect and draughtsman

James 'Athenian' Stuart to build life-sized replicas of his favourite ancient Graeco-Roman monuments. Stuart duly set about constructing the Tower of the Winds; the Lanthorn of Demosthenes; the Arch of Hadrian; and a Doric Temple. Easily the most enigmatic of the survivors, 'The Shepherd's Monument' is the one that concerns us most.

The Shepherd's Monument

Set originally in a rough 'alcove' or niche created in a wall of the orangery, the Shepherd's Monument is a marble bas-relief copy of seventeenth-century French artist Nicolas Poussin's most famous and enigmatic painting. Known both as *Les Bergers d'Arcadie* and *Et In Arcadia Ego*, its meaning is still open to interpretation. The Ansons commissioned the renowned Dutch sculptor Peter Scheemakers to make a new representation of the image in stone.

In Scheemakers' copy, as in the Poussin original, three shepherds and a woman gaze and/or point at a tomb inscribed with the words, '*Et In Arcadia Ego*'. The subject is taken from Virgil's *Bucolics* and before that from the *Idylls* of Theocritus. Both poets imagine an area of ancient Greece – 'Arcadia' – as a kind of rural Utopia whose inhabitants lived lives of guilt-less intellectual inquiry and sensual outdoor pleasure. In the Poussin painting, the shepherds seem to be making some kind of moral point about the 'I, too, am in Arcadia' motto. Most people believe this means that death is always among us, even in the midst of happiness; and that it paradoxically brings its own rewards. The monument is flanked by a pair of Doric pillars cut with a pattern of incised lines.

Why did Thomas Anson commission this monument? Was it at the Admiral's behest? Why, of all the paintings in the Western canon, did he ask the brilliant – and very expensive – sculptor Scheemakers to copy Poussin's *Et In Arcadia Ego* in the first place? The work has obvious resonance for a classical theme park of the type the Ansons were creating. But why that particular image? The obvious explanation is that Anson simply admired Poussin's work. The less obvious and more intriguing answer is that he wanted to hide something – and help the secret endure through the centuries by shrouding it in mystery. To this end, he asked Scheemakers to make a number of significant changes to Poussin's original. Taken together, these alterations can be read as a kind of code — but what does it mean?

The Stone Mirror

What is different? The scene has been reversed, right to left, as if we are viewing the image in a stone mirror. The standing female figure has entirely disappeared. A pyramid replaces the rectangular tomb; and what looks like an ornate funerary casket has been placed beneath its apex.

There is more: the angle of the two standing shepherds' staves or crooks is increased so that they now nearly conjoin. And looking very closely, we see that the head of the mythological Greek river god Alpheus has been cunningly worked into the rock formation directly beneath the shepherd on the monument's left side. In the myth, Alpheus has fallen in love with the beautiful nymph Arethusa, the daughter of Nereus, one of the Hesperides who look after a hidden paradise. To help Arethusa elude the river god's attentions, Artemis, goddess of chastity, turns her into a spring. But the cunning Alpheus even so possesses the nymph, by mingling his own much greater stream with hers.

There are at least two further alterations: the older, kneeling shepherd's hand has been repositioned in such a way that his thumb points to the letter 'R' in the word 'ARCADIA'. And then there is the mystery of the Shugborough Code itself.

The Shugborough Code

Scheemakers chiselled ten letters into the plinth beneath the bas-relief. Set out in this way –

O · U · O · S · V · A · V · V
D ·   M ·

– they make up a cipher known as the Shugborough Code. For more than 250 years, it has defied every attempt to solve it. Dickens and Darwin both tried and failed. More recently, Shugborough's management, in conjunction with Bletchley Park, the Second World War code-breaking centre that broke the top-secret Nazi Enigma code, organised an open competition. This attracted more than 130 entries. The winner was an anonymous American cipher expert who worked for a US government agency. He claimed to have discovered a numeric key – 1223 – scratched into the marble. This enabled him to decipher the message: JESUS H DEFY – the 'H', he said, derived from the Greek letter 'X', an abbreviation of the word *Christos*, 'Saviour'.

The winner claimed that this encoded 'Defy Christ' message links the Shugborough Code directly to the 'Priory of Sion', a secret brotherhood made famous by Dan Brown in his best-selling novel, *The Da Vinci Code*. In Brown's story, the Priory of Sion guards the Holy Grail: the secret knowledge that Christ was mortal, and not divine. He married and had a child by Mary Magdalene, and their sacred bloodline survives to the present day.

The Knights Templar were also said to be in on the secret. When they had control of the Jerusalem Temple, a chosen few removed the vital and potentially world-changing evidence of Christ's mortal bloodline from the undercroft. In one version of the story, this included Mary Magdalene's bones. King Philip II of France smashed the Templar order on Friday, 13 November 1307. As Philip's murderous henchmen closed in, the story goes on to tell us that a core group of knights escaped with the sacred knowledge. They took initial refuge in the ancient Albigensian fortress of Carcassonne, in southern France. From there, they dispersed either to Rosslyn Chapel in Scotland or to Nova Scotia in Canada, where they hid both themselves and their great secret.

Can we believe that the 'San Graal' of French writer Chrétien de Troyes's late fourteenth-century poem *Percival, the Story of the Grail* actually refers not to the cup of Christ, but to the 'Sang Real' or 'Royal Blood' of Jesus and the children he had with Mary Magdalene? Children whose descendants became the Merovingian monarchs of France from the fifth to the eighth century, and whose bloodline continues up to the present day?

Dan Brown starts *The Da Vinci Code* in this way: 'The Priory of Sion – a European secret society founded in 1099 – is a real organization.' In fact, at least in its original incarnation, the Priory of Sion was a hoax, concocted in the 1960s by Pierre Plantard and Philippe de Cherisey, two French adventurers looking to improve their fortunes. Plantard claimed he was Grand Master of the Priory of Sion. As such, he claimed he was the living incarnation of the Holy Blood, and a direct descendant of the Merovingian royal line. This made him not just the rightful heir to the throne of France, but the living embodiment of Christ's mortal bloodline on Earth. He has since died.

Brown backs up his story by citing a series of 'parchments' known as *Les Dossiers Secrets*. 'Accidentally discovered' in

France's prestigious Bibliothèque Nationale, these supposedly list the members of the Priory of Sion, who include Sir Isaac Newton, Sandro Botticelli, Victor Hugo and Leonardo da Vinci. In reality, and in an effort to lend their fraud credibility, the hoaxers planted the parchments in the French national library in 1967. A 2005 British TV investigation by actor and presenter Tony Robinson thoroughly exposed the deceit.

But if there is no Priory of Sion, then the anonymous American code-breaker's 2004 'solution' of the Shugborough Code competition is wrong, and the cipher remains unbroken. Are there any other clues to its meaning?

Numerous books, TV documentaries and articles have attempted to prove some connection between the southern French village of Rennes-le-Chateau, the Holy Grail, Poussin's *Les Bergers d'Arcadie* and buried Templar treasure. None is wholly convincing. But the Rennes-le-Chateau tale is quite fabulous. It involves a priestly murder; the Knights Templar; the Franks; the Visigoths; the Freemasons; Shugborough Hall; substantial caches of gold in the local countryside and just about anything else you can cram in.

One of the most entertaining ideas is that, if we can only unravel them, clues in the 'secret pentangular geometry' of Poussin's *Les Bergers d'Arcadie* provides the location to a fabled hoard of treasure. In this version of things, the Shugborough Code is the final piece of the puzzle that leads to the buried gold. Many have tried to solve the puzzle. No one has yet come away with the loot.

The Shugborough monument is dedicated to George Anson's wife, Elizabeth Yorke, daughter of Lord Chancellor Hardwicke. Anson family correspondence hints that Thomas was in love with his brother's 'coxcomb' wife. If true, then the Shugborough Code may have absolutely nothing to do with hidden treasure, Christ, Mary Magdalene, Rennes-le-Chateau or pentangular geometry. It may simply be Thomas Anson's own very personal way of commemorating Elizabeth. A quotation from the anonymous eighteenth-century 'Shugborough Poem' lends some weight to this interpretation:

> Let not the Muse inquisitive presume,
> With rash interpretation to disclose,
> The mystic ciphers that conceal her name.

This still does not explain all the alterations Thomas had Scheemakers make to *Les Bergers d'Arcadie*. However you care to shake them up, the letters D.O.U.O.S.V.A.V.V.M. don't work as an encoded version of the name 'Elizabeth'. A quote from one of his contemporaries tells us that Thomas Anson was 'much given to hanging over [the monument] in contemplation'. But that still doesn't help us decipher the code.

O · U · O · S · V · A · V · V

D ·   M ·

Does anyone have any idea what it means?

Atlantis

It's hard to believe that when he wrote down the story of Atlantis, philosopher, wrestler, misogynist and myth-builder Plato had any idea it would still be gripping the imaginations of people everywhere more than 2,000 years later. Yet this story of a drowned, long-lost city-state somewhere 'beyond the pillars of Hercules' has spawned more films, TV shows, books, articles, comics, video games and scholarly treatises than you can shake a *Symposium* at – and the fascination shows no signs of waning anytime soon.

Plato's original 360 BC treatises *Timaeus* and *Critias* are our only source for the Atlantis myth.

In these texts, we learn that the Greek statesman Solon visited the Egyptian goddess Neith's temple at Sais, in the Nile delta, in 590 BC. Here, Egyptian priests told him the story of a war between ancient Athens and a country known as 'Atlantis'. This, Solon said, had taken place 9,000 years before his visit. Plato says that Solon's Greek language translation is the only and unique source of the Atlantis narrative, and that 'the original writing . . . is still in my possession'.

The story goes that when the ancient Greek gods divided up the earth and the heavens among themselves, Poseidon, the sea-god, 'gained for his lot the island of Atlantis'. Poseidon didn't do too badly, as the territory he came to own 'once had an extent greater than that of Libya and Asia [Turkey] . . .'.

(Some believe the word 'island' in this context could equally well mean 'peninsula', or even 'island continent'.)

Plato tells us the new kingdom of Atlantis was mostly made up of mountains in the north. There was a great oblong plain in the south, 'extending in one direction three thousand stadia [555km; 345 miles] and two thousand stadia [370km; 230 miles] across the middle. Fifty stadia [9km; 6 miles] from the coast was a mountain that was low on all sides.'

Atlantis was the domain of Cleito, a human female. One day, 'Poseidon fell in love with her, and had intercourse with her; and breaking the ground, enclosed the hill in which she dwelt all round, making alternate zones of sea and land, larger and smaller, encircling one another; there were two of land and three of water, which he turned as with a lathe out of the centre of the island, equidistant every way, so that no man could get to the island, for ships and voyages were not yet heard of.' So a very long time ago, then, and before the age of navigation.

Cleito bore Poseidon five pairs of male twins. The eldest, Atlas, was appointed king, lending his name both to the island and to the surrounding seas, which we still know as the Atlantic Ocean.

Next, we're told the Atlanteans

> ... employed themselves in constructing their temples, and palaces, and harbours, and docks ... they bridged over the zones of sea which surrounded the ancient metropolis, and made a passage into and out of the royal palace; they began to build the palace and then the habitation of the god and of their ancestors. This they continued to ornament in successive generations, every king surpassing the one who came before him to the utmost of his power, until they made the building a marvel to behold for size and for beauty.

The eager citizens then dug huge canals, which gave the city access to the sea, and a harbour that entirely contradicts the statement that 'ships and voyages were not yet heard of'. The islanders used red, white and black stone in the construction of all these marvels. They then covered the outermost perimeter wall in brass, the next in tin, and the innermost, citadel wall 'flashed with the red light of orichalcum' – most likely copper.

Plato goes on to say that for many generations Atlantis was a moral, spiritual and technologically advanced civilisation with an amazing artistic culture. But its citizens were also mighty warriors: 'Now in the island of Atlantis there was a great and wonderful empire, which had rule over the whole island and several others, as well as over parts of the continent; and, besides these, they subjected the parts of Libya within the Columns of Heracles as far as Egypt, and of Europe as far as Tyrrhenia [Italy].' This military prowess immediately makes us wonder if the Atlanteans are the fearsome 'Sea Peoples' who are mentioned in a number of ancient Egyptian texts, who terrorised – and in most versions conquered – many of the states in the southern and eastern Mediterranean. Even Egypt itself, the superpower of the age, had to reach an accommodation with these early Mediterranean-style Vikings. The script on a *stela* (upright stone slab) in the temple city of Tanis reads: 'They came from the sea in their warships, and none could stand against them.'

Atlantis, then, was for centuries a kind of Utopia, and its people almost god-like in their wisdom, military might and moral virtue: '[F]or many generations, as long as the divine nature lasted in them ... they despised everything but goodness, not caring for their present circumstances, and thinking lightly on the possession of gold and other property, which seemed to them only a burden; neither were they intoxicated by luxury; nor did wealth deprive them of their self-control ...'

Then, in what reminds us of humanity's Biblical expulsion from the Garden of Eden, came the terrible fall: '[B]ut when this divine portion began to fade away in them, and became too often diluted . . . they, being unable to bear their fortune, became unseemly.'

Seeing that the Atlanteans had grown arrogant, greedy and immoral, the gods punished them 'by violent earthquakes and floods . . .' The end came 'in one single, fearful day and night' during which 'all the warlike men sank into the earth. The island of Atlantis likewise disappeared into the depths of the sea. And this is why the ocean in those parts is impassable, because a shoal of mud bars the way; and this was brought about by the island's subsidence.'

We have then, a quite detailed if tantalisingly incomplete description of Atlantis, its people, and its history. But why would we want to accept it as true? What makes any attempt to do this difficult is the frustrating lack of detail in the story. Where *exactly* was this sunken civilisation? Was it 'Dogger-land', the drowned land off the coast of south-east England that once linked Britain to the European mainland? There is no doubt that rising sea levels and/or the tsunami unleashed by the Norwegian Storegga Slide of around 6200 BC inundated this area. It is also 'beyond the Pillars of Heracles' and there is no shortage of mud shoals at the bottom of what are now the relatively shallow waters of the English Channel.

Or was this where the 'ideal' civilisation of the Mayans flourished before their doom? This was the pet theory of the US Congressman and writer Ignatius L. Donnelly (1831–1901). Donnelly's 1882 book *Atlantis, The Antediluvian World* did more to ignite modern interest in the subject than anything else. Like many others since, Donnelly viewed Atlantis as a 'precursor civilization'. Its artistic and engineering skills had provided the template for the ancient societies of the Americas,

Africa and Europe – and been especially influential in the creation of ancient Egypt. But then all of the wisdom and technological prowess Atlantis had given the world vanished in the Biblical Flood. Donnelly also had a personal axe to grind: Atlantis, he believed, was the original home of the red-haired, blue-eyed 'Aryans', whose descendants still lived in his Irish homeland.

The Nazis picked up on this profoundly wrong-headed idea and ran with it. In the years before the Second World War, Nazi 'Reichsführer' Heinrich Himmler set out to prove that all 'true' Germans were descendants of an ancient Aryan master race, and therefore superior to all other races. To bolster this poisonous notion, among other things they used passages from the Roman historian Tacitus. The big problem for Himmler was that no one had ever found any concrete evidence of the supposed ancient civilisation's actual existence or whereabouts. In this context, the story of Atlantis was a gift. It's a myth that can be all things to all people, and one that stubbornly refuses to be pinned down. Himmler's SS research teams, which included archaeologists and other scientific personnel who should have known a great deal better, travelled to Sweden, Scotland, Iceland, France and Tibet. They found nothing whatsoever to support the theory of Aryan or German racial supremacy.

Fuelled by strange, ancient 'cup and ring' carvings found at Laxe das Rodas, in the Doñana national park, a more modern theory places Atlantis in south-western Spain. Satellite imagery that appears to show traces of an ancient concentric settlement near a beach in the area, as well as of other, long-ruined rectangular buildings, added to the debate. Experts remain divided over whether these traces do in fact provide evidence of Plato's concentric city-state – but this part of Spain is also well 'past the Pillars of Hercules'.

There are many other supposed locations for the drowned land. Most are islands in or near the Mediterranean Sea, and include Sardinia, Crete, Santorini, Sicily, Cyprus, and Malta. Land-based cities or states such as Troy, Tartessos, and Tantalus, in the province of Manisa, Turkey, also enter the lists, as does Israel-Sinai. The Black Sea, the Sea of Azov, the 'Bimini Road' or 'Wall' off the Bahamas, and the Southern Ocean off the coast of eastern South Africa also feature as candidates.

If we are going to speculate about the location of a mythical lost land, then geology is a factor worth bearing in mind. Many scientists believe that, as the vast ice sheets of the last Ice Age began to melt some 19,000 years ago, global sea levels rose by a total of more than 120 metres (394 feet). This melting lasted until about 6,000 years ago, which means that the average rate of sea-level rise during the long, slow period of warming was roughly one metre per century. There were even greater, periodic 'jumps' in sea level at varying locations, as we have seen for example in the English Channel. In this context, a civilisation that lasted for a few thousand years before being drowned and buried deep by the sea is perfectly possible.

Few scientists believe that Atlantis was real in the first place, although American historian and professor Charles Hapgood used the story to push forward thinking about plate tectonics. In his 1970 book *The Path of the Pole*, Hapgood proposes the idea that 'the outer shell of the Earth shifts from time to time, moving some continents toward and other continents away from the poles . . . This book will present evidence that the last shift of the Earth's crust [the lithosphere] took place in recent time, at the close of the last Ice Age, and that it was the cause of the improvement in climate.' If the Earth's crust 'slipped like an orange peel around the segments of an orange', as Hapgood put it, then it is quite possible that an ancient island continent was swallowed in the mix. Even better, the dates he cites roughly coincide with Plato's 9000 BC.

In his 1966 book *Maps of the Ancient Sea Kings*, Hapgood proposes that ancient maps – the 1513 Ottoman Piri Reis map being a big contender – provide concrete evidence of 'an advanced worldwide civilization that existed many thousands of years before ancient Egypt'. This is all extremely good fun, but unfortunately for Hapgood, modern geology came along and disproved his theories.

What does the science of the past have to say about Atlantis? One hot day in 1967, Greek archaeologist Professor Spyridon Marinatos had a flash of insight. Marinatos, who had helped explore world-famous sites such as Marathon and Thermopylae, was excavating a villa at Amnisos, just east of the Cretan capital Heraklion. He looked down. The matter between his fingers wasn't earth. What was it that he had been continually scraping away at for all these days and weeks? Up until that time, most archaeologists believed that an earthquake had destroyed Crete's Bronze Age palaces. Yet the Amnisos villa's entire interior was filled with volcanic pumice. Surely this meant that, as at Pompeii, Crete had suffered the effects of a volcanic eruption?

If so, then how? There is no volcano on Crete. Where was the nearest one? For years, Marinatos had nursed the theory that there could be an ancient settlement on the nearby island of Santorini. No one had ever found any trace of it – but the crescent-shaped main island did feature a dormant volcano. At some time around 1625 BC, the geological evidence showed that this had erupted, blowing the heart out of what was then known as Thera. The ash and smoke that billowed out into the atmosphere following the explosion was so great that contemporary scribes as far away as Egypt and even China recorded changes in the weather.

Marinatos spent ten years leading digs on the island of Santorini. Persistence pays off, and eventually he struck archaeological gold. There, buried beneath a thick layer of volcanic debris, lay the ancient Minoan city of Akrotiri. Complete with dazzling murals depicting the daily lives of the people who had lived there until the catastrophic explosion buried and miraculously preserved much of it, Akrotiri depicts a civilisation at peace both with itself and with its neighbours. The many wonderful images portray a Utopia of the kind Plato describes, in which people concentrated most on the business of enjoying themselves.

If Atlantis ever was a real place, then Santorini is a prime candidate for its location. The island was circular (it only became a crescent when it was blown apart), and the excavated houses depicted in the murals stacked neatly against the ancient hillside are made of red, white and black local stone, precisely fitting Plato's description. This was of course mythical, but may be the echo of a folk-memory. In the wake of the eruption, the neighbouring population of Minoan Crete was hit by one of the biggest tsunamis the world has ever seen. The wave that smashed across the island is believed to have towered as high as 30 metres (100 feet), racing in and devastating the coastal settlements where most people lived.

In 2016, National Geographic produced *Finding Atlantis*, a television documentary whose aim was to investigate new theories about the location of the 'real' Atlantis. The following year, in the Strait of Gibraltar, a separate documentary team working in association with National Geographic and led by film-maker James Cameron found a cluster of six 4,000-year-old stone anchors.

Was Plato's Atlantis the vehicle for a purely allegorical tale about the dangers of hubris and social corruption, aimed squarely at the Athens of his day? Or will we ever discover any solid scientific evidence that it really existed? One thing is for certain: the idea of an ancient civilisation lost beneath the waves is so brilliant and so powerful that the search for Atlantis is likely to keep on going for as long as we do.

The Bermuda Triangle

The ten years between 1940 and 1950 were spectacularly bad for aircraft flying through the 'Bermuda Triangle'. Often defined as the area enclosed by imaginary lines joining Miami, Bermuda and Puerto Rico, it covers more than 500,000 square miles. Also sometimes known as 'The Devil's Triangle', this huge patch of sea and the airspace above it has earned a reputation as a deadly graveyard for ships, aircraft and people. Many articles and books have claimed there is some kind of paranormal cause for the multiple disappearances, suggesting they are the result of anything from alien activity to sea monsters to kidnap by raiding parties from the lost city of Atlantis surfacing to snaffle some fresh blood.

The modern excitement about the Bermuda Triangle seems to have gained critical mass in February 1964, when a journalist named Vincent H. Gaddis published an article with the headline 'The Deadly Bermuda Triangle' in *Argosy* magazine. Picking up on earlier speculative articles by Associated Press reporter Edward van Winkle Jones and George X. Sand, Gaddis claimed that only what he called the 'hoodoo of the triangle' and 'the mysterious menace that haunts the Atlantic off our south-eastern coast' could explain the number of ships and aircraft that had inexplicably disappeared in the area.

In an article published in 1991, *Time* magazine reported that there had been more than a hundred unexplained disappearances of aircraft and ships in the previous 45 years. While Gaddis may have helped spark the modern fascination, triangle fear has been around for a lot longer: in September 1492, Christopher Columbus reported seeing 'strange lights in the heavens', as he passed through the area, and recorded that his ship's compass needle was swinging wildly instead of remaining on magnetic north.

Of the many unaccountable losses in the Bermuda Triangle, the case of Flight 19 has provoked the most fevered speculation and drawn the most persistent media attention. Shortly after 2 p.m. on 5 December 1945, five US Navy Grumman TBM Avenger torpedo bombers took off on a routine navigation-training mission from US Naval Air Station Fort Lauderdale, Florida. Weather and visibility were good. Led by Flight Instructor Lt. Charles Carroll Taylor, a Second World War veteran who had flown more than 2,500 hours and many combat missions in the Pacific, Flight 19 numbered 14 men in total. All of the pilots were fully qualified and had already flown between 300 and 450 hours each, of which at least 55 hours were on the TBM Avenger.

The weather over Fort Lauderdale was bright and sunny, and the forecast for the training area was described as 'favourable'. There might be some scattered rain showers, with surface winds of between 20 and 31 knots, and the cloud ceiling within the showers was predicted to be 2,500 feet, but it would be clear outside any showers. Sea state was moderate to rough. It was winter, and there was nothing extreme or in any way unusual about these conditions, and nothing to stop the navigation exercise from going ahead.

Nicknamed the 'Iron Bird' on account of its durability, the TBM was, and remains – a few are still flying – a big, robust, three-seater aircraft engineered to withstand enemy fire and high-impact carrier landings. Pilots in the Second World War said it flew like a truck, but that wasn't necessarily intended as a criticism.

The aircraft that made up Flight 19 were four TBM-1Cs – BuNo 45714, 'FT3'; BuNo 46094, 'FT36'; BuNo 46325, 'FT81'; BuNo 73209, 'FT117' – and a single TBM-3, BuNo 23307, 'FT28'. The 'BuNo' was the aircraft's Bureau, or serial number, while the 'FT' number is painted on the tailplane. All five aircraft were fully fuelled at take-off. But in each case, the aircraft's cockpit clock had for some reason been removed. Since the purpose of the navigation exercise was, among other things, to teach the principles of dead reckoning, their omission is odd – but may just have been down to nothing more sinister than routine maintenance. Since all aircrew wore wristwatches as a matter of course, the absence of the onboard clocks was not viewed as a problem.

Assigned to complete 'Navigation Problem No. 1', Flight 19 was scheduled to fly almost due east that day for 56 nautical miles (64 miles; 104km); bomb Hen and Chickens Shoal, a rocky shelf that lies near Bimini, about half-way between the Florida Keys and the Bahamas, en route; continue on east for a further 67 nautical miles (77 miles; 124km); turn north onto heading 346 degrees for a further 73 nm (84 miles; 135km); then turn south-west onto heading 241 degrees and fly back home to base. On the face of it, the mission was straightforward, not to say easy – a three-sided triangle that should have caused none of the trainee navigators any great problem to complete. Even if one of the fledgling airmen managed to lose track, the flight's very experienced instructor would simply take over the lead and shepherd them back onto the right course. All aircrew were briefed to fly in formation close enough to maintain visual contact with one another at all times.

At about 1315, shortly before the time of their scheduled

departure, something odd happened: Lt. Taylor reported to the Aviation Training Duty Officer and asked to be excused from the mission. He gave no reason, other than to say that he 'did not want to take this one out'. The duty officer told Taylor there was no available replacement, especially at that short notice.

Each pilot had to dead reckon individually using the compass airspeed and elapsed time between the navigational legs. One or the other might be required to lead the flight on a given leg, or for part of a given leg. To this end, for the initial leg Lt. Taylor adopted the rearmost position in the flight in order to track progress, while one of the students took the lead.

In order to check their navigation was correct, and to help pilots stay on course and return safely to base, the two major waypoints of the flight – the points at which they should have made their major turns – were deliberately over and within sight of land (visibility always permitting). To help make sure they did spot these landmarks, the flight maintained a relatively low altitude throughout.

The first waypoint, at the termination of the outbound, easterly leg of the scheduled flight from Fort Lauderdale was over the north-western tip of Great Stirrup Cay. Here, whoever was leading Flight 19 at the time, it should have turned north onto 346 degrees, and flown on a further 73 miles to waypoint two. This second leg took the flight directly over the easterly quadrant of Grand Bahama Island, which is too big to miss, unless you really can't see anything at all. Yet while the weather was beginning to worsen, visibility should not yet have been a problem. Following this second visual check of their position with reference to a landmass, the flight continued on for another 15 miles or so before reaching its final waypoint. This was also within sight of a large island, in this case, Great Sale Cay. Having sighted this final landmark, and once again used it to verify their location, the trainees should have made their final turn onto 241 degrees and headed for home.

The flight definitely made it as far as Hen and Chickens Shoal, because a radio transmission from one of the pilots was picked up at 1500 hours asking for permission to drop the last of his bombs. Taylor told him, 'Go ahead and drop it.'

Forty minutes later, when the flight should have been at or near Great Sale Cay, the senior US Navy flight instructor at Fort Lauderdale, Lieutenant Robert F. Cox, who was about to lead a separate group of navigation trainees on the same 'Navigation Problem No. 1' mission, overheard a disturbing message. One member of Flight 19 was transmitting on 4805 [kilocycles – the common training frequency] to 'Powers' [this was Captain E. J. Powers, US Marine Corps]. The unknown caller repeatedly asked Powers what his compass was reading. After a long delay, Powers responded, 'I don't know where we are. We must have got lost after that last turn.'

On hearing this, Cox informed Fort Lauderdale control that either a ship or an aircraft was lost, he did not know which. He then sent a message to Powers: 'This is FT 74 [Cox's call sign]. Plane or boat calling "Powers", please identify yourself so someone can help you.' There was no reply. Then the same voice Cox had initially heard came back on, this time definitely identifying as 'FT 28' – Lt. Taylor. Cox sent: 'FT 24, this is FT 74, what is your trouble?' Taylor, who had by now taken over as flight leader, replied: 'Both of my compasses are out, and I am trying to find Fort Lauderdale, Florida. I'm over land but it's broken. I'm sure I'm in the Keys but I don't know how far down, and I don't know how to get to Fort Lauderdale.' If he really was over the Florida Keys, then Taylor and the rest of the flight were between 150 and 175 miles from where they should have been – and in serious trouble.

Fort Lauderdale control heard some of the exchanges

between Cox, Taylor and the other Flight 19 pilots. But inter-ference from Cuban radio stations, static, and the generally poor atmospheric conditions meant that radio reception was patchy overall. The weather in the Bahamas region was now reported as worsening, with low cloud and poor visibility.

The standard operating procedure for aircraft lost in the Atlantic near the US coast was to turn west onto 270 degrees and steer for land, using the sun as a guide if you could see it, and otherwise relying on the compass, your dead reckon-ing skills, your common sense, and your experience. Instead of turning west, and apparently convinced he was somewhere over the Gulf of Mexico, Taylor told the flight to steer north-east. This took it on a track out into the North Atlantic.

Taking Taylor at his word, and believing the flight to be over the Florida Keys, and not any of the Cays north of Grand Sale, Cox told him to 'Put the sun on your port wing and fly north up to Fort Lauderdale.' It may have been given in the best possible faith, but as events were to prove, it was terrible advice.

At 1626, Air-Sea Rescue Task Unit Four (ASRTU-4) based at Fort Everglades heard a fresh transmission from Lt. Taylor: 'I am at angels 3.5 [3,500 feet]. Have on emergency IFF. Does anyone in the area have a radar screen that could pick us up?' ASRTU-4 contacted Fort Lauderdale, who notified Naval Air Station Miami and more than 20 other bases to try and locate the lost flight. The 'emergency IFF' or Identification Friend or Foe radio transponder on all the Flight 19 aircraft including Taylor's should have made this reasonably straight-forward. But no facility or unit could get an accurate fix on the five TBMs.

At 1645, Taylor radioed: 'We are heading 030 degrees for 45 minutes, then we will fly north to make sure we are not over the Gulf of Mexico.' In reality, he was nowhere near the Gulf – and heading north-northeast was simply taking the flight out further into the Atlantic Ocean. At 1703, he transmitted: 'Change course to 090 degrees for ten minutes.' This was taking the flight in the exact opposite direction to Fort Lauderdale. If, as many have suspected, Taylor had mistaken some of the Bahamanian Cays for the Florida Keys, then he was leading everyone astray. At least one of the other pilots, sensing the mistake, keyed his radio: 'Dammit, if we would just fly west, we would get home, dammit.' He was right.

At the end of a few more anxious minutes, the other pilots persuaded Taylor to turn west. But when they still didn't sight land, and with darkness beginning to fall, shortly after 6 p.m Taylor, still apparently believing they were somewhere in the Gulf of Mexico, went back on his decision again: 'We didn't go far enough east. We may as well just turn around and go east again.'

At this point, shore-based triangulation came up with a rough but critical fix on Flight 19's position: they were north of the Bahamas and east of Florida, as by now almost everyone bar Lt. Taylor believed. By some great sin of operational omission, none of the land bases, ships or aircraft that were by now trying to locate Flight 19 thought to transmit this information 'blind' or continuously on all available channels. As a result neither Taylor, nor any of the other pilots, ever learned where they actually were.

At 1820, as Flight 19 began running out of fuel, Taylor was faintly heard ordering the trainees to get ready for ditching: 'All planes close up tight. We'll have to ditch unless landfall . . . when the first plane drops below ten gallons, we all go down together . . .' At almost the same time, the captain of the British oil tanker *Viscount Empire*, which was to the north-east of the Bahamas en route to Fort Lauderdale, told ASRTU-4 that a full storm was now blowing in the area, with very high seas and gale-force winds.

Taylor and another student, possibly Capt. Powers, now took turns in leading the flight, and the aircraft zigzagged hopelessly to and fro across the Atlantic. In the end, as their fuel ran out, in the darkness of a December night and horrendous weather conditions they had to ditch. All five aircraft and all 14 men aboard them disappeared without a trace.

Their loss sparked a huge sea and air search-and-rescue mission. The first three aircraft to start looking for the Avengers were a PBY Catalina seaplane and two PBM Mariner flying boats. One of the Mariners, PBM-5 BuNo 59225 from Naval Air Station Banana River (now Patrick Air Force Base) took off into the winter night at 1927 with 13 crewmen aboard.

A few minutes later, BuNo 59225 transmitted a routine radio message reporting its position. This gave no hint of any problems with the aircraft. At 2115, the oil tanker SS *Gaines Mills* – which had no connection with any of the military aircraft, and was on a routine voyage – reported seeing the fireball of a very big explosion at position 28.59°N 80.25°W. A pillar of flame shot up into the sky, towered to 100 feet (30m) and burned for ten minutes. It is now believed that this sighting marked the mid-air explosion of BuNo 59225, which stopped responding to radio messages and vanished at that exact time. Despite making full speed to the probable crash site and conducting a thorough search, the SS *Gaines Mills* found no traces of the Mariner or any of its crew.

Coming directly after the loss of Flight 19, this second disappearance supercharged the mystery of the Bermuda Triangle. How could six modern US military aircraft all disappear on the same day, without any explanation? Many people, both at the time and ever since, believe that something very strange indeed must have been at work. The more sceptical commentators reasoned that the PBM Mariner was known to suffer vapour leaks when fully laden with fuel, prompting aircrews to call it the 'flying gas tank'. Given that it disappeared off the radar at the same time as the fireball sighting, the simplest and most logical explanation is that, true to its wholly undesirable reputation, BuNo 59225 exploded in mid-flight.

As dawn broke on the following day, the US Navy despatched more than 300 ships and aircraft to search for Flight 19 and the PBM Mariner. They searched over both land and water for five days, but found no sign of any bodies, petroleum slicks or wreckage.

In a poignant coda to the incident, in May 1991 a salvage team searching for lost Spanish galleons discovered all five torpedo-bombers only ten miles (16km) off the coast of Fort Lauderdale, Florida. They had almost made it home.

Two Avro Tudor IV airliners operated by British South American Airways also went missing in the 1940s. The first, call sign G-AHNP *Star Tiger*, vanished somewhere in the area on 30 January 1948 with 31 passengers and crew.

Sister aircraft G-AGRE *Star Ariel* disappeared a little less than a year later, on 17 January 1949, flying between Bermuda and Kingston, Jamaica. Whereas *Star Tiger* had been battling terrible weather conditions and had probably been blown too far off course to make landfall before its fuel ran out, *Star Ariel* went missing in fine weather. The subsequent air accident investigation speculated as to whether some of the characteristic communications problems that seemed to dog the region had contributed to the *Star Ariel*'s disappearance. Adding to the sorry list of unexplained losses in the Bermuda Triangle, it concluded that, 'through lack of evidence due to no wreckage having been found, the cause of the accident is unknown.'

On 28 December 1948, a Douglas DC-3 Dakota airliner

carrying 26 people on a flight from San Juan, Puerto Rico to Miami went missing 50 miles from its destination, once again in the suspect area. Following a final call to confirm it was approaching the airport, and in a pattern that by now had become only too familiar, the DC-3 and all 32 people on board it vanished and were never seen or heard from again. In this case, the Civil Aeronautics Board investigation concluded there was 'insufficient information available on which to determine probable cause of the disappearance'.

Another case that is sometimes cited as evidence of malign paranormal activity in the Bermuda Triangle is the March 1918 disappearance of the USS *Cyclops*. This very large freighter's entire crew of 308 men and her cargo of 11,000 tons of manganese ore disappeared somewhere between Barbados and Baltimore. No distress call was ever received from the ship, and an extensive search once again found no sign of any wreckage. Commenting on the loss, President Woodrow Wilson said, 'Only God and the sea know what happened to the great ship.'

The subsequent and very similar disappearances of two of USS *Cyclops'* sister ships, USS *Proteus* and USS *Nereus* may, though, provide a more prosaic explanation for the loss of these bulk carriers: catastrophic structural failure. Overladen and with their I-beams corroded by the action of the manganese ore they routinely carried, all three may simply and without warning have snapped in two and sunk, going down so fast there was no time for anyone on board to send a distress message.

There are many, many more examples of ships and aircraft going missing in the Bermuda Triangle, too many to mention in anything other than a dedicated book; but as we've seen with some of the above examples, when you start to scrutinise them closely, in just about every case there is an element of ambiguity.

On the one hand, the disappearances can seem so strange and sudden as to defy all rational explanation; on the other, later and more modern research can throw up possible and more prosaic reasons for their occurrence.

This has not stopped the flood of publications claiming the losses in general as phenomena beyond the explanation of any and all conventional science. Among the wilder theories that have been put forward is the idea that all the people who have gone missing in the Bermuda Triangle (and perhaps even their ships and aircraft) have been seized by the denizens of Atlantis, the sunken city Plato was the first to mention in his 360 BC discourses, *Timaeus* and *Critias*.

Writer Charles Berlitz even proposed that the city of Atlantis was itself a victim of the Bermuda Triangle. In this account, once the Triangle had swallowed them up, the Atlanteans decided to maintain their numbers by kidnapping innocent passing travellers. They achieve this by means of some nefarious and advanced technology, which they themselves have developed. Quite how the snatched human souls manage to stay alive beneath the sea is not fully explained.

One of the supposed locations of Atlantis is the very same Bimini Road rock formation that Flight 19 bombed on the day it went missing. Bombing a lost civilisation probably annoys its citizens no less than bombing one that is currently up and running. In both cases, the civilisations in question are likely to strike back.

In a suspiciously neat tie-up with the Great Pyramid of Giza, some theorists propose that the Atlanteans harness the power of 'fire crystals' operating in the same harmonic register as Khufu's monument to communicate across an invisible but powerful global matrix. This may be entertaining, but even in a world that sometimes struggles with the truth, it may also not be entirely a matter of fact.

Another of the more audacious theories claims that aliens are responsible for all the disappearances, snatching unsuspecting travellers from the Bermuda Triangle for the purposes of more or less unwholesome experiments. Why the Bermuda Triangle, instead of anywhere else in the world? One answer put forward is the presence of a Top Secret US Navy facility at Fresh Creek on the Andros archipelago in the Bahamas.

Officially known as the Atlantic Undersea Test and Evaluation Center, AUTEC is the underwater equivalent of Nevada's Area 51. It is used for US maritime forces special operations training, weapons testing and sonar research. An imaginative interpretation of AUTEC's remit proposes that, as at Area 51, the US government is working covertly with extraterrestrials. The aim is to develop secret super-weapons, which will afford the United States and its alien allies joint global and interplanetary dominance. To further the research, innocent air and sea passengers navigating the Triangle are captured and used as guinea pigs in outlandish and gruesome experiments.

Passengers on cruise ships have reported sighting UFOs in the Bahamas area. We should note only in passing that strong cocktails are available on board these remarkable vessels at all times.

To counter claims that supernatural, extraterrestrial or paranormal activity are the cause of the losses in the Bermuda Triangle, sober and professional scientists have put forward a number of more rational explanations. Not least among these is simple human error: pilots and mariners sometimes go unprepared and ill equipped for the conditions they might meet in a region renowned for its volatile weather. They also make catastrophic navigational mistakes, which may or may not have been what happened in the case of Flight 19. They get drunk, fight with one another at the controls, and generally mess up.

A 2016 Norwegian investigation came up with the idea that

giant methane bubbles erupting without warning from enormous pockets of gas trapped beneath the sea floor may have caused aircraft and ships to disappear. These methane bubbles rise to the surface, then pop, creating an air pocket that engulfs unsuspecting maritime and air traffic, a bit like a Great White shark snapping up a surfer.

Then there's the area's unpredictable and sometimes violent weather. Hurricanes, cyclones and sudden squalls all feature in its formidable arsenal. Tropical storms in which lightning strikes and atmospheric electrical disturbances can produce serious compass anomalies, radio interference and machinery failure are also common. Ball lightning, which may explain the 'strange lights' Columbus recorded in his log, is also a local speciality, and let's not forget the towering and voracious waterspouts that rise up from nowhere and scud across the sea. You would not want to fly through one of those.

What about sudden downdraughts of very cold air? A US National Hurricane Center satellite specialist tells us that, 'during very unstable weather conditions, the downburst of cold air from aloft can hit the surface like a bomb, exploding outward like a giant squall line of wind and water.' Scientists are also currently trying to find out if 'hexagonal clouds' might be producing these 'air bombs'.

All of these climatic conditions can of course occur in many other parts of the world, and not just in the Bermuda Triangle. And while they can cause ships and aircraft serious and sometimes fatal problems, maritime insurance marketplace Lloyd's of London does not count the Bermuda Triangle as one of the planet's most dangerous places. In 1997, a Lloyd's spokesman said, 'There are just as many losses [in the Bermuda Triangle] as in other wide expanses of ocean', adding that Lloyd's insurance premiums for transits through the area were no higher than they were for any other routine sea voyages. To the insurance industry the sea is a dangerous environment, wherever you happen to sail.

The US Coast Guard service agrees with Lloyd's, stating that: 'In a review of many aircraft and vessel losses in the area over the years, there has been nothing discovered that would indicate that casualties were the result of anything other than physical causes. No extraordinary factors have ever been identified.' In a random example, the US 7th Coast Guard district reports that in 1975, 21 ships disappeared unaccountably and without trace off the coast of the United States – but that of these, only four vanished in the Bermuda Triangle. Given that the seas in the area are among the busiest in the world, with more than 150,000 vessels of all sizes passing through them annually and upwards of 10,000 calls every year for help, the Coast Guards say that if anything, they're surprised losses in the Devil's Triangle are not substantially higher.

In 1975, chief Bermuda Triangle sceptic, pilot and sometime Arizona librarian Lawrence Kusche wrote *The Bermuda Triangle Mystery – Solved*. He followed that book up in 1980 with a new title, *The Disappearance of Flight 19*. A meticulous researcher, Kusche combed through hundreds of official documents, personally overflew the Flight 19 route and conducted first-hand interviews with key witnesses to investigate more than 50 of the reported losses in the area. The evidence he came up with goes a long way towards demolishing the notion that any of the ship and aircraft losses in the Bermuda Triangle are in any way mysterious.

If Kusche is right, then the 'Mystery of the Bermuda Triangle' may be nothing more than a figment of an opportunistic journalist's imagination. Once the story gained traction, the theory is that a flood of sensational books and articles meant that people started noticing – and recording – losses in the region much more diligently than they did anywhere else in the world. No one seems to have done a comparable study on the losses of aircraft, ships and lives in a similar area of the world. Does an element of doubt about the Bermuda Triangle persist in spite of this? What do you think?

The *Mary Celeste*

'. . . a sad and silent mystery of the sea . . .'

Here is a fine ship, newly refitted, her slim prow cutting the Atlantic swell in clean style. Driving along under full sail, the half-brig describes a long, slow, corkscrew, plunging fast as she rolls to starboard, before rushing up to teeter on the back of the next wave. The motion delights little Sophia Briggs. Aged two-and-a-bit, she bounces on the upper deck, shouting for glee when the ship's downward travel leaves her weightless for a catch, and then shrieking for joy when the deck races back up again and forces her to curtsy. Chattering and making up games, she entrances the crew.

Her mother, Sarah Elizabeth, whose letters are filled with love for her child, and give us a snapshot of a bright, engaging little button, keeps Sophia on a tight rein. The child is at the least cautious age. The ship's wooden gunwale, which encloses the upper deck, is low: the sea rushes past a few feet below where they stand. Sometimes, when the Atlantic decides to put a random spoke in its own rhythm, the *Mary Celeste* hits the water hard: a great surge breaks high over the bows, exploding into millions of tiny droplets that catch the sun and then burst in a thousand rainbows, before whipping down to spray mother and child with a stinging hail. Still, they must have fresh air and take some exercise: as the weather grows ever warmer, the captain's cabin feels increasingly close.

Twenty days out of New York, the merchant ship is nearing the Azores Islands, and making good speed towards Gibraltar. Sophia's father, Captain Benjamin Spooner Briggs, is pleased with their progress: every day, he writes in his log that all is well. On 25 November 1872, he makes one last entry: 'At 8, Eastern point bore SSW 6 miles distant.' Briggs means the eastern point of St Mary's Island, the most easterly and southerly of the Azores archipelago, and he is talking about eight o'clock in the morning.

It is the last anyone will ever hear of Sarah Elizabeth; of the irrepressible Sophia Matilda; of Captain Briggs; and of the *Mary Celeste*'s seven crew. The ship will go sailing on without them. And no trace or sign of them will ever be found.

How can we possibly begin to explain this mystery? On the morning of Tuesday, 5 November 1872, the *Mary Celeste* slipped her moorings at New York's Pier 50, East River dock and set sail for Genoa via Gibraltar. Under the command of the 37-year-old Captain Briggs, the ship was laden with a cargo of pure alcohol. The spirit was stored in 1,700 stoppered wooden barrels stacked three or four deep, fore-and-aft in the hold, and chocked with wooden wedges to prevent them from shifting at sea.

The weather was bad, so Briggs decided to anchor off Staten Island for two days until it improved. This meant that the *Mary Celeste* did not actually begin her transatlantic voyage until the morning of 7 November. The vessel's Master was an experienced merchant sea captain with many successful voyages to his name. His wife, Sarah – she was also a cousin – had sailed with her husband on previous voyages, but little Sophia Matilda was new to the sea. The couple's seven-year-old son, Arthur Briggs, remained behind with his paternal grandmother at the family home in Marion, Massachusetts.

Judging by the letters Briggs and Sarah wrote in the days before the voyage, everything about it was perfectly normal. They were looking forward to a profitable outcome: Benjamin Briggs had purchased an 'eight-twenty-fourths' interest in the ship; and as well as making good money from the delivery of the alcohol on behalf of Messrs. Meissner, Ackerman and Co., wine merchants, the *Mary Celeste* had already been booked to carry a cargo of fruit from Messina to New York on the return voyage. Mrs Briggs, a keen amateur musician and singer, had made sure to have her precious melodeon installed in her husband's cabin before departure.

The *Mary Celeste*'s crew comprised:

First Mate: Albert G. Richardson, 28, who had served honourably during the American Civil War from 1864–65 in Company A, Coast Guard Infantry, Maine Volunteers. Richardson had also served previously under Captain Briggs.

Second Mate: Andrew Gilling, aged 25.

Steward and Cook: Edward William Head, 23. Newly married when the half-brig sailed, Head was 'respected by all who knew him', according to the *Mary Celeste*'s majority owner, Captain James H. Winchester.

All four remaining members of the crew were German and enlisted as seamen. They were:

Volkert Lorenzen, 29.
Boz Lorenzen, 25, his brother.
Arian Martens, 35.
Gottlieb Goodschaad, 23.

The German members of the crew all came from solid, God-fearing backgrounds, and on any assessment appear to have been the salt of the earth. Their respective families – which included young children – relied on them to send home regular remittances from their earnings, and would be devastated if anything happened to their breadwinners. There is no record or evidence that any member of the crew was of anything but excellent character, and plenty that they were uniformly trustworthy.

Eight days later, on 15 November, a second ship, the brigantine *Dei Gratia* also left New York harbour. The two vessels were very similar in size and type, and, like Benjamin Briggs, the *Dei Gratia*'s 34-year-old captain, David Reed Morehouse, was looked on as a first-rate seaman. Born at Sandy Cove, Novia Scotia, Morehouse went to sea aged 16. Quickly showing exceptional prowess in navigation and seamanship, he won his first command of a merchant ship at the age of 21.

Coincidentally, the *Dei Gratia* was also headed for Gibraltar on the first leg of her voyage, laden with a cargo of petroleum. At the time of sailing, the *Dei Gratia*'s captain was 'on orders', which means the shipping company would only tell Morehouse where he was to deliver the fuel once he arrived in Gibraltar. At the time, this way of going about things was perfectly normal.

In order to reach Gibraltar, both ships had to pass the Azores, which lie some 2,570 miles (4,136km) to the east of New York and far out in the Atlantic Ocean. By any standards, the Azores are remote: continental Portugal, the nearest mainland, lies 850 miles (1,360km) to the east. The coast of Africa is 936 miles (1,507km) away; and Newfoundland, Canada, is 1,196 miles (1,925km) to the north-west. Any way you look at the map, the Azores archipelago is surrounded by thousands of square miles of empty, open sea.

Despite this, at about 1 p.m. on Wednesday, 4 December 1872, and 19 days into his crossing, Captain Morehouse sighted another ship.

The Sighting

Morehouse took out his telescope. The more he studied her, the less he liked the look of the other vessel, which was scudding along about four miles away on the port, and windward, bow. To his nautical eye, the set of her sails looked thoroughly wrong: only the unknown vessel's jib and forward staysail were set, while the lower fore-topsail was flapping loose in the wind. Loose, flapping sails are a bad sign on any sailing ship – a symptom either of sloppy seamanship, or trouble. Some of her rigging also looked awry. There were lines trailing over the sides and she was yawing – veering from side to side as if no one was at the helm and holding her on a steady course. Although she was not flying any distress signals, Morehouse decided the stranger might be in need of help, and ordered his crew to haul up on her. As they drew near, they saw a name picked out in white on her black-painted transom: *Mary Celeste*.

'Ahoy, brigantine *Mary Celeste*,' Morehouse hailed. 'Are you in need of assistance?' No one was visible on deck, and there was no reply. Stranger still, there was no one at the ship's helm: although she was making slow forward progress on the starboard tack, the *Mary Celeste* appeared to be sailing without any sign of human help. The set of her sails and the wind direction meant that, at the time of her discovery, the *Mary Celeste* was heading roughly north-west, back towards the United States – and not east towards Gibraltar.

While the *Mary Celeste*'s sails and rigging were not in regular order, there was no evidence of any serious damage either to them or to the ship as a whole. This was all very unusual, to say the least. By now, all seven members of the *Dei Gratia*'s crew were on deck with the captain. Like him, they were utterly mystified: why was nobody on the other ship responding to their repeated calls? Why was there no sign of anyone? Where was her crew?

Morehouse ordered three men to launch one of the boats and row across to investigate. First Mate Oliver Deveau and Second Mate John Wright clambered into the longboat and stood on the oars, while ordinary seaman John Johnson took the tiller. Following a short if vertiginous crossing on the back of some steep waves – the wind had freshened recently and the swell was still building – Deveau and Wright climbed aboard the stranger. Johnson remained alongside in the boat, in case the other two ran into any trouble and they all had to make a quick escape. There was no reason yet to expect foul play – but there was also no way of knowing what they might find aboard.

The first thing Deveau did on boarding was to call out, in the hope of finding someone alive. The next thing he did, like a good seaman, was to examine the ship's pumps: he was already beginning to suspect the vessel had been abandoned. If true, then surely her captain must have believed that she was sinking?

She wasn't. The first mate found both pumps in good working order. There was, though, an anomaly: one of the pump mechanisms had been 'drawn' – that is, removed from its housing – to allow the sounding rod to be lowered. This meant that someone had been trying to check the depth of water in the hold. Deveau found it lying on the upper deck, but he could not use it at once because the rod in question was already wet. This suggested either that one of the vessel's crew had used it recently, or that sea spray had drenched it.

Deveau now followed Wright and began exploring the ship. Moving slowly through the silent passageways and cabins, they neither saw nor heard a living soul. Spotting a length of line with a bolt tied to the end of it lying in the First Mate's cabin, Deveau lowered it down the pump housing. When he drew it back up, it told him there was about three-and-a-half feet of water in the hold. It was a significant amount, but with two working pumps, it should be nothing to worry about: all sailing ships of the time took in water in the course of a long sea voyage. It was a routine matter to keep it under control with the pumps.

Continuing his search, Deveau found more seawater in the 'forward house' – the broad, low structure housing the cabins that projected up through the foredeck – and yet more sloshing around between decks. This sounds as if it might be more serious, but it wasn't: the ship was not flooded, unmanageable or sinking. If there had been anyone left on board, then any excess seawater would have been quickly cleared.

Deveau noted that the fore hatch and the lazarette (aft storage) hatch had been removed and left alongside their respective coamings. This would have allowed salt spray and rain to penetrate below, and no doubt served to explain some of the flooding. There was no explanation for anything else that was going on in the *Mary Celeste*. The binnacle – the wooden cabinet that houses the ship's compass – had been knocked off its stand and was damaged, and the compass itself was smashed beyond repair.

The ship's foresail and upper fore-topsail had apparently been blown away in the rising gale, and the lower fore-topsail was 'hanging by the four corners'. The main-staysail had been hauled down and left lying in a heap on top of the forward house. The jib and forward staysail were still set on the starboard tack, and it was these that accounted for the ship's bedraggled attempt to return home, like a horse that has been let loose and is trusting to instinct. All the other sails were furled, and although there were some ropes hanging loose over the sides, the great majority of the standing rigging, including the gaffs and the peak halyards, remained intact.

Rope lashings and fenders had been secured across the *Mary Celeste*'s main hatch, suggesting that a longboat might have been attached to it. But if there really had been a boat, and if it had been launched as an emergency lifeboat, then that must have been done by manhandling it over the ship's side. There were no davits, or small cranes, on the ship. It was quite possible to launch a small lifeboat with six or seven strong crewmembers, but Deveau and Wright had no way of knowing whether that had actually happened. What they had established was that there was no one else aboard. To both men, their tour of inspection left them utterly bewildered: as experienced seamen, they judged the *Mary Celeste* seaworthy. Yet she had been abandoned. Why?

The more they tried to work out what might have happened, the more the mystery deepened. The ship's essential navigational aids were nowhere to be found: the captain's chronometer, which was needed to establish longitude; the sextant, which could be used for finding both longitude and latitude; the navigation book; the ship's register and other important papers were all missing from the captain's cabin. The log book – a diary of the ship's position, course, speed, and any other important events – was in the first mate's cabin, while the log slate, used to create a rough account before the fair record was entered into the log book proper, was lying on the table. In his cabin, the two men found items of clothing that suggested a woman and a small female child – almost certainly his immediate family – had been travelling with the *Mary Celeste*'s captain. This was poignant – and made the matter of the ship's abandonment even more unsettling.

There was no cooked food in the galley or anywhere else on the ship, but Wright and Deveau found enough provisions in the storeroom to last for six months, and plenty of clean drinking water. There was no table laid with food and drink that had been left there in haste – but this would later make for a good story.

They saw no signs of violence on the ship, and no signs of a fire or an explosion in the hold. No one seemed to have tampered with the valuable cargo of alcohol.

Half an hour or so after boarding, Deveau and Wright clambered back into the longboat and returned to the *Dei Gratia*. They told Morehouse that the volume of water in the ship was not so serious that some work at the pumps would not correct it, and that the damage to her sails, rigging and other gear could be mended in short order. As far as both men were concerned, and both were highly experienced sailors, the ship was perfectly workable and could be 'sailed around the world' following this remedial work. The question Morehouse put to them repeatedly was the only one they couldn't answer: why, given that she could be worked, had the ship been abandoned?

The *Dei Gratia*'s captain and crew now began a lengthy discussion. All eight men knew that, as an intact vessel, the *Mary Celeste* on her own had to be worth a considerable amount in salvage money. On top of that was her liquid cargo, which, once delivered, would also fetch a handsome sum. If they were to deliver her intact, the ship's insurers would surely be prepared to reward them.

First Mate Oliver Deveau proposed taking command of the abandoned vessel, and sailing her on to Gibraltar with two of the *Dei Gratia*'s crew. The rest of the hands backed him. This presented Morehouse with a difficult decision. Given that one man must be at the wheel and on watch at all times, under no circumstances was three men enough to sail the *Mary Celeste* in perfect safety. Leaving only four men to crew the *Dei Gratia* also broke every rule of common sense and safe navigation. It was mid-winter, and there were still 600 miles (965km) of open sea between their present position and Gibraltar. The wind had not abated, and the seas were still running high. All of Morehouse's experience and good sense made him reluctant to agree with Deveau's proposal. Yet there was the potential prize, bobbing peacefully along a couple of cables away, waiting to be turned into cash.

If they were to leave the ship drifting helplessly and sailed on, they would gain nothing. Should they risk losing both ships, in the hope of gaining the salvage reward for one?

At last, Morehouse made up his mind. Deveau would take Able Seamen Charles Lund and Augustus Anderson, and sail the *Mary Celeste* on to Gibraltar. The men were delighted. Hopping to it, Deveau and his salvage crew took with them the *Dei Gratia*'s small boat, a compass, a watch, a barometer and some food for immediate consumption. The risk was slightly mitigated by the fact that Deveau had commanded a brig once before; he was an accomplished navigator and proficient in the use of his personal sextant.

At about four o'clock on the afternoon of 4 December, Deveau, Anderson and Lund boarded the abandoned vessel and began repairs. By nine o'clock that evening, they had pumped out most of the excess water, fitted a spare trysail in place of the missing foresail, made running repairs to the rigging and set the remaining sails to suit the prevailing conditions. With the *Dei Gratia* in close company, the *Mary Celeste* once again turned her slim nose towards Gibraltar and got underway.

At first, all went well: the weather improved and the two ships remained within sight of each other. Then, with little warning, they hit a storm in the Strait of Gibraltar. This separated them. The *Dei Gratia* made the better going of it, docking on the evening of 12 December. Captain Morehouse now endured a full day and night of high anxiety, pacing the long harbour wall that juts far out from under the shadow of the immense Rock as he waited for the other ship.

He need not have worried: the *Mary Celeste* reached harbour early on the morning of Friday, 13 December. The date is reckoned unlucky, and in this case, it was: on the orders of T.J. Vecchio, Marshal of the Vice-Admiralty Court, the port authorities seized the salvaged ship the moment she tied up alongside. Given the apparent loss of life, and the oddly intact condition of the ship, Vecchio also ordered an immediate official enquiry.

Almost everything we know about *Mary Celeste*'s discovery, her condition at the time of the encounter and all the facts of her apparent abandonment and salvaging are taken from the official testimonies that Captain Morehouse, First Mate Deveau and the six other men of the *Dei Gratia*'s crew made in the course of this investigation. The problem is, we don't know if they were telling the truth.

On 18 December 1872, the Gibraltar Admiralty Court met to begin hearing the case for the salvage of the *Mary Celeste* brought by the *Dei Gratia*'s owners and the ship's company. This was officially recorded as: 'The Queen, in her office of Admiralty Against the Ship or Vessel supposed to be called Mary Celeste and her cargo proceeded against as derelict.'

Enter a man with a somewhat improbable name: Frederick Solly Flood. From the very first, the Queen's Advocate made it clear that he suspected the *Dei Gratia*'s crew of foul play. He did not believe the meeting of the two ships could possibly have been a matter of chance. In collusion with one or more members of the *Mary Celeste*'s crew, they must have enacted a violent and preplanned conspiracy. The motive was obvious: to profit from the salvage money. Further, to Flood's way of thinking, the *Mary Celeste* could not possibly have travelled the 600 or so miles (965km) from her last position as recorded in the log book without a crew. And certainly not to the location where the *Dei Gratia* had discovered her. In his view, some or all of the men now ranged before him in court had enacted a plan to make it look as if the *Mary Celeste* had been abandoned, recover her as if by chance, and then share in the salvage money.

The first witness to be called before the court was Oliver Deveau. Deveau told the story much as it is set out above, but in much greater detail. Jumping about from one point to the next, and not always sticking to the questions put to him, the First Mate did nothing to allay Solly Flood's suspicions:

The wind during the last four days before we found the vessel was north-westerly. The men's clothing was all left behind: their oilskins, boots, and even their pipes, as if they had left in a great hurry or haste. My reason for saying that they left in haste is that a sailor would generally take such things, especially his pipe, if not in great haste . . .

I found the fore-hatch and the lazarette hatch both off; the binnacle stowed in, a great deal of water between decks – the forward house full of water up to the coaming. The forward house is on the upper deck. I found everything wet in the cabin in which there had been a great deal of water – the clock was spoilt by the water – the skylight of the cabin was open and raised – the compass in the binnacle was destroyed.

I found all the captain's effects had been left – I mean his clothing, furniture, etc. – the bed was just as they had left it – the bed and the other clothes were wet. I judged that there had been a woman on-board. I found the captain's charts and books, a number of them, in the cabin – some were in two bags under the bed and some two or three loose charts over the bed. I found no charts on the table.

I found the logbook in the mate's cabin on his desk – the log slate I found on the cabin table. I found an entry in the logbook up to 24th November, and an entry on the log slate dated 25th November showing that they had made the island of St Mary. I did not observe the entry on the slate the first day, and made some entries of my own on it, and so, unintentionally rubbed out the entry when I came to use the slate; at least, I thought I did. I did not find the ship's register or other papers concerning the ship, but only some letters and account books . . .

In his cabin hanging over the mate's bed showing the track of the vessel up to the 24th there were two charts – one under the mate's bed and one, as I have said, hanging over it. I am not positive whether the chart with the ship's track marked on it was found above or below the mate's bed. There seems to be everything left behind in the cabin as if left in [a] hurry, but everything in its place. I noticed the impression in the captain's bed of a child having lain there . . .

The whole of the vessel appeared in good condition and nearly new. There were a great many other things in the cabin, but impossible for me to mention all – the things were all wet. The skylight was not off but open, the hatches were off, the cabin was wet but had no water in it . . . the water had naturally run out of it . . . the masts were good, the spars all right, the rigging in very bad order – some of the running rigging carried away, gone – the standing rigging was all right – the upper fore-topsail and fore-sail gone, apparently blown away from the yards. Lower foretopsail hanging by the four corners . . . the vessel I should say it was seaworthy, and almost a new vessel. Anchors and chains all right. There were no boats and no davits at the side. I don't think she used davits. It appeared as if she carried her boat on deck. There was this bar lashed across the stern davits, so that no boat had been there . . .

Flood was now even more certain that violence had played a part in the affair. His conviction grew into obsession. He embarked on a ferocious cross-examination of Oliver Deveau, hoping to catch him out in a lie. But Deveau was not easy to shake. Harry and probe as Flood might, the First Mate responded with the same, if somewhat entangled, account. Rather in the manner of a dentist drawing an especially recalcitrant tooth, Flood did, though, extract some useful extra information:

We spoke [with] one other brigantine on our voyage, bound for Boston, but did not pass or see any other vessel of a similar class on our outward voyage. Therefore, the first time we could have seen this vessel was the day we found her as we did – deserted. I cannot say without referring to my Log, where our ship was on the 24th or 25th. I do know we were to the north of the other vessel. I know that we were between latitude 40° and 42°. I only know that we were north of the vessel from seeing her track traced on her chart.

We did not sight St Mary's Isle during any part of our voyage. I do not know the latitude longitude of St Mary without seeing a chart. I have made only one voyage from New York to Gibraltar before, and did not sight St Mary's then. I never was at St Mary's – never saw it . . .

. . . One could see whether boats had been lashed across the main hatch, but that was not the right place for her. There were no lashings visible; therefore, I cannot swear that the *Mary Celeste* had any boat at all, but there were two fenders where the boat would be lashed . . .

My idea is, that the crew got alarmed . . . that they had sounded the pumps and found perhaps a quantity of water in the pumps at the moment – and thinking she would go down, abandoned her.

At this point in Deveau's testimony, the clerk produced Exhibit C, the *Mary Celeste*'s chart. The First Mate said:

The chart now produced is the chart I found on board the *Mary Celeste* with the ship's course marked on it. I used it afterwards myself, for our track here. The words written: '*Mary Celeste*, abandoned 5 December 1872' are in my writing . . . that chart is the chart I found in the Mate's cabin. We passed to the north of the [Azores Islands] group – the *Mary Celeste* passed to the south . . .

I should say that, from the spot marked on the chart as the last position of the *Mary Celeste* on the 24th up to the place where we found her . . . would be from 500 to 600 miles. The only explanation of the abandonment, which I can give, is that there was a panic from the belief that the vessel had more water in her than afterwards proved. I cannot give an opinion as to whether the derelict could have run the distance [to] where we found her in the interval with the sails she had set. [The interval of eleven days between the *Mary Celeste*'s position as last recorded in her log, and the point where the *Dei Gratia* found her.] She was going steadily from 1½ to 2 knots when we saw her, with the wind on her beam. She might have had more sails set at first. She would not run steadily before the wind with her rudder unlashed . . .

The water casks were on chocks. The chocks had been moved as if struck by a heavy sea. The provision casks were below in their proper place: they were not thrown over. If the vessel had been capsized, they would have been thrown over.

The testimonies of John Wright, the *Dei Gratia*'s Second Mate, and of the other crewmen echoed Deveau's more or less exactly. The court heard the last witness on 20 December. Even though their testimonies agreed in sum and in detail – and possibly because of that – nothing any of the crew said helped convince the court officials they knew what had actually happened on board the *Mary Celeste*.

As news of the strange case started to spread, 'The Mystery of the Mary Celeste' began to fascinate the world. Wild fabrications began circulating as fact. With the exception of Sophia Matilda, everyone involved fell under suspicion.

On 23 December, Flood and the court as a whole were surprised and angered to learn that the *Dei Gratia*, which had been in port since 12 December, had cast off and sailed with her cargo of petroleum for Genoa. Her captain was none other than the key witness in the case, Oliver Deveau. The *Dei Gratia*'s final destination, only recently revealed to Captain Morehouse 'under orders', was the same as the *Mary Celeste*'s. This further coincidence increased the doubt in the minds of Flood and many others. Morehouse remained behind in Gibraltar, in case, as he put it, he was required to deal with any other issues that might affect the court's decision.

On the same day, still determined to prove his theory of foul play, Advocate Flood led an inspection of the *Mary Celeste*. Flood, Marshal Thomas J. Vecchio, a Surveyor of Shipping, John Austin, and a local diver named Ricardo Portunato spent several hours examining the derelict inside and out. Wright and Deveau had both sworn they'd found no trace of violence, or of blood anywhere on board. Then, and in a moment of drama that to Flood proved that all of his suspicions were justified, Marshal Vecchio found a sheathed sword. It was lying on the deck of the captain's cabin. Why had none of the *Dei Gratia*'s crew reported it to the court?

Now even more convinced that murder had played a part in the story, on 7 January Flood made 'a still more minute examination for marks of violence', this time accompanied not just by Vecchio, but by no fewer than four Royal Naval captains and a colonel of the Royal Engineers. In a letter to the London Board of Trade, Flood states:

From the survey it appears that both bows of the derelict had been recently cut by a sharp instrument but that she was thoroughly staunch sound and strong and every way seaworthy and well found, that she was well provisioned and that she had encountered no seriously heavy weather and that no appearance of fire or of alarm of fire or explosion or any other assignable cause for abandonment was discoverable. A sword however was found which appeared to me to exhibit traces of blood and to have been wiped before being returned into the scabbard . . . On examining the starboard topgallant sail [spar] marks were discovered apparently of blood and a mark of a blow apparently of a sharp axe. On descending through the forward hatch a barrel ostensibly of alcohol appeared to have been tampered with . . . [Deveau and Wright, we remember, had not noticed this in the course of their initial examination of the ship.]

The working Chart and the ship's log were also found . . . complete up to noon on 24 November . . . the deck or slate log is continued . . . up to 8 a.m. on the following day, at which hour the eastern point of St Mary's [Azores] bore south-southwest distant six miles – she had therefore run considerably less number of knots since the previous noon than that entered on the Slate . . . Since then eight weeks have elapsed, and nothing whatsoever has been heard of the Master or Crew or of the unhappy Lady and Child . . .

My own theory or guess is that the crew got at the alcohol, and in the fury of drunkenness murdered the master whose name was Briggs and wife and Child and the Chief Mate – that they then damaged the bowels of the Vessel with the view of giving it the appearance of having struck on rocks . . . and that they did sometime between 25 November and 5 December escape on board some vessel bound for some north or south American port or the West Indies . . .

Unfortunately for Frederick Flood, none of this stood up. Examined forensically, the 'traces of blood' on the sword turned out either to be rust or some other form of corrosion. Flood retorted that the blade had been 'wiped with lemon' to remove the traces of blood, but by now few people were taking him seriously.

In a further blow to the Advocate's theory, the *Mary Celeste*'s cargo of alcohol was found to be in pure form, and so poisonous unless heavily diluted. This meant that, even if they did break a barrel open and indulge in a drunken binge, the *Mary Celeste*'s crew were much more likely to die or fall ill than they were to start rampaging through the ship with murder in mind. The marks on the ship's topgallant rail also proved not to be bloodstains. The six-foot long, three-eighths-of-an-inch deep cuts to both sides of the *Mary Celeste*'s bows did remain a mystery, at least in so far as the Surveyor of Shipping, John Austin, was concerned. In his statement, he said: 'this injury had been sustained very recently and could not have been effected by the weather and was apparently done by a sharp cutting instrument . . .' These twin cuts on her bows remain one of the strangest unresolved details of the mystery.

A new actor, Captain R.W. Shufeldt, now enters the scene. Shufeldt, who commanded the United States Ship *Plymouth*, arrived in Gibraltar on 5 February. At the request of Horatio Sprague, the US Consul in Gibraltar, Shufeldt carried out a new survey of the *Mary Celeste*. She was, after all, an American ship, and her owners, as well as several of the missing passengers and crew, were United States citizens.

Captain Shufeldt went about his work with exemplary speed and efficiency. In his report he states:

> I am of the opinion that she was abandoned by the master & crew in a moment of panic & for no sufficient reason . . . I reject

the idea of mutiny, from the fact that there is no evidence of violence about the decks or in the cabins; besides the force aft and forward was so equally divided, that a mutiny could hardly have had such a result.

The damage about the bows of the Brig appears to me to amount to nothing more than splinters made in the bending of the planks – which were afterwards forced off by the action of the sea . . .

If surviving, the Master will regret his hasty action. But if we should never hear of them again, I shall nevertheless think they were lost in the boat in which both Master and crew abandoned the *Mary Celeste* and shall remember with interest this sad and silent mystery of the sea . . .

One of Flood's other main reasons for suspecting mutiny or hijack was the distance the *Mary Celeste* had run between the time of her supposed abandonment on 24 November, and the moment of her supposed discovery, on 5 December. Flood reasoned that, with the prevailing wind 'more or less from the North' she must, for most of that interval, have been running on the port, and not the starboard tack. If true, this meant she could not have sailed so great a distance westwards 'upon the starboard tack'.

In one of several letters to the London Board of Trade, Flood stated: 'These circumstances lead me to the conclusion that although no entry either in the Log or on the slate of the *Mary Celeste* later than 8 a.m. on the 25th of November is to be found, she had in fact not been abandoned till several days afterwards, and probably also that she was abandoned much further to the Eastward than the spot where she was found . . .'

Nothing could shake Flood's belief that some or all of the *Mary Celeste*'s crew had mutinied, killed others aboard including the captain and his family and then somehow disappeared;

or, that the *Dei Gratia*'s crew had murdered everyone on board the derelict so as to gain the salvage reward.

With no one at her helm, it is impossible to say what course the *Mary Celeste* followed during the crucial period; she might have changed direction more than once of her own accord, and even at an average speed of 1½ knots, it was quite possible that she had made the 600 miles or so westward.

Deveau successfully delivered the *Dei Gratia*'s cargo to Genoa on 16 January 1873. She then sailed for Messina. This again was the same port for which the *Mary Celeste* had originally been bound to pick up her return cargo of fresh fruit. The word 'coincidence' begins to seem a little overused.

While the *Dei Gratia* was in Genoa, the Gibraltar court summoned Deveau to testify for the last time. He returned to Gibraltar by steamship, and took the stand – it must by now have been very familiar to him – on 4 March 1873. Flood had a final go at his least favourite witness, again extracting details Deveau had not previously mentioned. The most important of these concerned the sword:

> I saw no remains of a painter or boat's rope fastened to the rail. I did not notice any mark of an axe on the rail or cut . . . I cannot say how the cut came in the rail – it appears to have been done with a sharp axe, and I do not think it could have been done by my men whilst we were in possession of the vessel. I did not see any new axes on board the *Celeste*; there was an old axe we found on board . . .
>
> I observed no marks of blood on deck. I noticed no marks or traces of blood upon the deck. I cannot say whether there were any or not; we never washed the decks of the *Mary Celeste* nor scraped them. We had not men enough for that. The sea washed over the decks. [At this point Flood told the court that salt water contains chloric acid, which dissolves blood.]

... I found that sword [he pointed to the exhibit lying on the court table] under the Captain's berth ... there was nothing remarkable on it. I do not think there is anything remarkable about it now – it seems rusty. I think I put it back where I found it or somewhere near there. I did not see it at the foot of the ladder – perhaps some of my men may have put it there. I was not on board ... when the Marshal came on the *Celeste* to arrest the vessel, and therefore I did not see him find the sword.

Two things stand out in Deveau's testimony: on first entering the cabin of John Wright, the *Mary Celeste*'s First Mate, he says: 'I found an entry in the Log Book up to 24th November, and an entry in the Log Slate dated 25th November showing that they had made the island of Saint Mary. I did not observe the entry on the slate the first day, and made some entries of my own on it, and so, unintentionally rubbed out the entry when I came to use the slate; at least, I thought I did.' Given how important any entries on the logs were and still remain in getting to the bottom of the mystery, Deveau's uncertainty remains a cause for concern.

Deveau goes on board a drifting ship; discovers that she's been deserted in great haste; finds an edged weapon under the captain's bunk, and can't remember if he altered the log slate. How eerie must that initial search through the chambers of a ghost ship have been? And how memorable?

Are we, even so, to believe that Deveau was a double-dyed villain, who concealed his leading role in a vicious and cynical massacre? If so, then it was pretty stupid of him to leave the sword lying around instead of chucking it into the sea, and then fail to mention it in court. The very fact that he was so casual – and forgetful – about it works in his favour. And always, we come back to the lack of any blood trace or marks of violence.

Deveau's final testimony concluded the case. With a new

Master and crew, the *Mary Celeste* left Gibraltar on 10 March 1873, arriving in Genoa on 21 March 1873 and discharging her cargo 'in good order'. The ship's principal owner, Captain James H. Winchester, had sailed across from New York to find out what had happened to his ship. Winchester had been fretting in Gibraltar for several weeks, and must have been mightily relieved when the Admiralty Court ordered that the *Mary Celeste* be released: he would now receive the payment of $3,400 – equivalent to £65,000 in 2018 money – for delivering the alcohol. Whether he also received any reward from the separate insurance of £6,522 3s 0d on the half-brig's cargo is not known.

What, then, really happened aboard the *Mary Celeste*? The penultimate entry in the ship's log on the morning of 25 November states: 'at 5 o'clock [0500], made the Island of S. Mary's, bearing ESE.' In sailor talk, this means the ship was within sight of land. Three hours later, we remember that the final entry on the log slate reads: 'At 8 [0800], Eastern point bore SSW 6 miles distant.' There is nothing in either entry to indicate an emergency on board the ship during the intervening timespan, and no mention of the deteriorating weather.

If we believe the record, the *Mary Celeste* made track of about 20 miles (32 km) around the northern coast of St Mary's in the space of these three hours. At 8 o'clock, the ship's speed is recorded as being eight knots, which roughly adds up with the distance logged. It also suggests that all sails were correctly set and that the ship was proceeding normally. After that, there is nothing. The story of the *Mary Celeste* ends in a silence that has lasted for the best part of 150 years.

There was no sea mist to obscure visibility or scatter the senses on 25 November, and in the morning the winds were light. But as the day wore on, the weather deteriorated, until a full gale blew up in the afternoon. Did the seas grow so rough as to make Captain Briggs fear that the ship might founder? If that were the case, then why was there not more water in the ship when she was found, and more damage to her rigging and cargo? And why did someone leave two of the upper-deck hatches open to the storm?

Six miles is not so far to row for eight able men taking turns at the oars. But if they did decide to launch the longboat in response to some emergency and strike out for Santa Maria, what happened to them?

Any sailor would know that taking to a small boat in rough seas is a bad idea: there is every chance the craft will be swamped, drowning everyone. For reasons of sheer size and mass, any seaworthy ship generally has a much better chance of surviving a storm than a small boat. Briggs would hardly have risked the lives of his wife and child, as well as his own, without some very good reason.

All kinds of theories have been put forward over the years, some intelligent, others less so, to explain the mystery. One leading contender is that there was an explosion of some kind, caused by vapour leaking from one or more of the barrels of alcohol. This theory was first put forward by Dr Oliver Cobb, cousin to both Captain and Mrs Briggs, and a man who, unable to accept their unexplained disappearance, was determined to find out what had happened to his relatives.

Cobb reckoned that, because of the generally poor weather the *Mary Celeste* encountered before reaching the Azores, the crew had kept her hold tightly sealed. As the ship sailed south and the air temperature increased, Cobb reasoned that alcohol fumes that had leaked from one or more of the casks warmed up, expanded, and became more volatile. Known as 'the angel's share', such leakage from stored volatile compounds was difficult to contain, not least when it was stored in wooden barrels.

Then, either two of the metal hoops that bound the barrels accidentally knocked together creating a spark, or one of the crew went into the hold with a naked flame. Whatever caused the ignition, in Cobb's version of events the ethanol fumes exploded with an almighty bang, terrifying everyone on board and triggering the abandonment.

The officials who inspected the vessel in Gibraltar flatly contradict Cobb's explanation. All agree there was no evidence of any explosion or fire. But were they right? In 2006, Professor Andrea Sella of University College London's Chemistry Department decided to test Doctor Cobb's theory under conditions of modern scientific rigour.

Sella asked his colleague Marty Jopson to build a replica of the *Mary Celeste*'s hold. Substituting cubes of paper for the wooden casks, they filled the space with butane, which is no less volatile than ethanol, retired to a safe distance and ignited it. The gas exploded with a loud 'whoomph'. A great ball of flame roared through the space. The explosion also blew open both hatches in the roof of the model hold. Commenting on results that might otherwise baffle those of us who are not scientists, Prof. Sella said: 'We produced a fuel and air explosion that creates a strong pressure wave. There was a spectacular wave of flame, but behind it was relatively cool air. No soot was left behind and there was no burning or scorching.' Adding weight to Dr Cobb's theory, Sella concludes: '[T]his replicates conditions on board the *Mary Celeste*. The explosion would have been enough to blow open the ship's hatches and would have been completely terrifying for everyone on board.'

Scared witless by the sound and fury of the blast, then, and fearing that the entire cargo would now explode, Captain Briggs gave the order to abandon ship. While two or three of the crew raced to shorten sail, the others ran to the longboat.

Once it was launched, everyone climbed aboard and rowed it away at top speed.

Cobb believed that when they clambered into the longboat, one of her crew tied it to the *Mary Celeste* by means of a long length of rope. The fugitives paid out this line until they felt they were at a safe distance from what they took to be a ship on the point of exploding. Although unmanned, the *Mary Celeste*, with its sails trimmed so as not to make too much speed and put them at increased risk from the rising seas, then towed them along. Everyone in the lifeboat watched anxiously for signs of a fire or a second explosion. When nothing happened, they should have simply pulled themselves back to the ship and returned aboard. Then, having checked to make sure the cargo was no longer in danger of exploding, they could have continued their voyage in safety. Instead, as Cobb proposes it, the heavy seas whipped up by the sudden gale snapped the towrope. Unable to pull themselves back, they were then at the mercy of the rising seas. A wave swamped the lifeboat and everyone subsequently drowned or died of exposure.

The theory is persuasive, but remains unproven. If they couldn't use the rope because it had snapped, why didn't they simply row back? Or had they forgotten to take the oars?

What else might have happened? That stalwart of seafaring yarns, the giant kraken, inevitably features in some of the wilder, fictional accounts of what happened to the *Mary Celeste*. There is no scientific proof that anything larger than the giant or colossal species of octopi exists – no remains of a squid-like creature big enough to attack and perhaps even sink a sizeable ship have ever been found. But we know very little indeed about the very deep ocean, and there are more things under heaven and the sea than we can perhaps dream of.

In his epic science-fiction novel *20,000 Leagues Under the Sea*, Jules Verne has a squid big enough to qualify as a kraken attack Captain Nemo's submarine, *Nautilus*. The submarine has to surface and fight with the monster in order to chase it off. For his part, in his 1830 sonnet *The Kraken*, the Victorian English poet laureate, Alfred Lord Tennyson, leaves us with a haunting account of the mythical creature:

> Below the thunders of the upper deep;
> Far, far beneath in the abysmal sea,
> His ancient, dreamless, uninvaded sleep
> The Kraken sleepeth: faintest sunlights flee
> About his shadowy sides; above him swell
> Huge sponges of millennial growth and height;
> And far away into the sickly light,
> From many a wondrous grot and secret cell
> Unnumber'd and enormous polypi
> Winnow with giant arms the slumbering green.
> There hath he lain for ages, and will lie
> Battening upon huge seaworms in his sleep,
> Until the latter fire shall heat the deep;
> Then once by man and angels to be seen,
> In roaring he shall rise and on the surface die.

Female giant squid (they grow bigger than the males) can grow up to 13 metres in length – but the idea that even a creature this big could suddenly rear up from the depths, envelop a vessel of the *Mary Celeste*'s size and snatch the entirety of her crew demands a very great suspension of disbelief. Let's imagine for a moment that a kraken did swim up from the deep, grab the helmsman on watch and anyone else who was on the upper deck in its tentacles and make to drown them. Then, as the others heard the screams and confusion of the victims, did they race topsides to find out what was happening, only to be seized in their turn and dragged to their deaths? The one possible piece of supporting evidence for this is the cut mark on the ship's rail. Did someone try to chop off a gigantic tentacle, as everyone scrambled for the lifeboat?

Pirates? A bit late for that, in 1872, in the middle of the Atlantic. Even at their peak, sea-thieves tended to loiter near ports, or hang along well-established trading coasts, on the lookout for easy prey. Alien abduction? Again, we enter the realms of the absurd. An iceberg? The local Azores weather records discount it, and we are very far south even for the roguest of growlers. Or did one of the crew suddenly become insane, butcher or shoot everyone on board and then throw himself into the sea?

How about Solly Flood's conviction that there was either a mutiny or some kind of pre-arranged conspiracy? As we've seen, all the official testimony and evidence is stacked against it.

If it were simple mutiny by some or all of her own crew, and an ensuing massacre, then where did the mutineers go once they had seized the ship? Why would they not have remained on board a perfectly seaworthy and valuable vessel, sailed it to some remote destination, sold the ship and its cargo to the highest bidder and then disappeared with the money they'd made?

What about the theory that Briggs and Morehouse knew one another beforehand? Let's assume that when they were in New York prior to sailing, the two captains met and hatched a plan to fake the abandonment. When they were within sight of the Azores, the *Dei Gratia*'s men took control of the *Mary Celeste*. In this version of events, the ghost ship's passengers and crew then rowed on to St Mary's, and waited in this remote and god-forsaken spot for their share of the salvage money. But as they were heading for landfall a flash storm blew up, swamped the longboat, and drowned the lot of them. The *Dei Gratia*'s crew then made the best of a bad outcome, and sailed both ships on to Gibraltar.

Would Captain Briggs really have risked his wife and daughter in such a hazardous conspiracy, when he had only just purchased a legitimate third share in the ship? Would the honest and God-fearing Mrs Briggs have agreed to be part of such a scheme? Neither seems very likely.

Let's suppose the good ships *Dei Gratia* and *Mary Celeste* met by simple coincidence. The captains exchanged pleasantries, and Briggs invited Morehouse and a couple of his men – perhaps Deveau and Wright – to come aboard for a noggin. Suddenly realising they had an opportunity to make money, the *Dei Gratia*'s men set about the *Mary Celeste*'s passengers and crew, slaughtered every one of them including Sophia Matilda, and threw the bodies into the sea. They then sailed both ships on to Gibraltar as before.

The prior longstanding good character of the *Dei Gratia*'s men militates against it. So too does the enormous risk in sailing two brigs a further 600 miles, with only four men manning one ship, and three the other. If the storm that overtook them had hit before they were relatively safe in the Strait of Gibraltar, both vessels and everyone aboard them might easily have been lost.

The amount of the salvage reward could not in any case have been accurately known in advance. In such cases, payments depend on the court believing an honest salvage has taken place to begin with, and even then the sum to be paid out is discretionary. In the case of the *Mary Celeste*, while the ship and her cargo were insured to a total of $17,400, and the value of her cargo assessed as £6,522 3s 0d, the final reward for her salvage came to a mere $1,705. This had to be split between the *Dei Gratia*'s owners and her crew. The evidence suggests that none of the parties involved were pleased either with the payment, or with its distribution.

Finally, and as we've seen, while a gale did blow up on 25

November, like all her type the half-brig was built for open ocean sailing and should have weathered anything bar the most severe gale or typhoon, neither of which is mentioned in the Azores weather reports. A seaquake, then, in which a huge void suddenly opened up and swallowed the ship? We simply can't say.

In the wake of the disaster, many opportunists and charlatans claimed to have been on board the *Mary Celeste* before she was found, or to have special inside knowledge concerning the mystery. All of these were more or less blatant attempts to make money from the disaster; achieve celebrity; or both. All have been shown to be false.

Even the great Sherlock Holmes author Sir Arthur Conan Doyle got in on the act. In 1884, the 25-year-old Doyle anonymously published *J. Habakuk Jephson's Statement* in the *Cornhill Magazine*. While it was based on the true story of the *Mary Celeste*, Doyle's story is almost entirely fictional. He peoples the vessel – now known as the '*Marie Celeste*', a change of name that has stuck to this day – with characters of his own invention. One of these, 'Septimus Goring', is the villain of the piece. Goring somehow interferes with the ship's course, so that instead of gaining its intended destination of Lisbon, it ends up off the coast of West Africa. Here, Goring and three crewmen overpower and gag the narrator, the eponymous Mr Jephson. Signalled from the ship, more members of the criminal conspiracy then paddle out from the shore in canoes, kill the rest of the crew and leave the vessel drifting and abandoned. With the ship's legitimate crew members despatched, the renegades make for a nearby settlement, which Septimus Goring intends to rule as an absolute monarch. No longer of any use to Goring, Jephson is now about to be murdered in his turn.

He survives because of the 'strange black stone' he carries. Doyle's unreliable narrator says this was given him before he embarked on the *Marie Celeste* by Martha, an old, black female slave who nursed him of the injuries he suffered while fighting on the Union side in the American Civil War. Martha tells Jephson she is grateful for his service to slaves in the Abolitionist cause, and would like him to have the stone as a reward. By an almighty stroke of luck, not to mention one of the most extraordinary coincidences to feature even in Victorian literature, it turns out that the stone Martha gave Jephson exactly fits into a socket in the head of a deeply venerated statue in the settlement Goring intends to rule. 'In a moment converted from a prisoner into a demi-god,' Jephson is freed and Goring helps him escape.

Absurd though it is in almost every detail, the yarn is told so persuasively that many, including even some of the more serious newspapers, considered it a true record. Frederick Solly Flood did not share in the general enthusiasm: '*J. Habakuk Jephson's Statement*,' he thundered, 'is a fabrication from beginning to end.' Also taken aback by its reception as fact when he knew it was not, US Consul Sprague asked *Cornhill Magazine* to tell him who had written the yarn. As far as we know, the magazine protected its source.

While the disappearance of the eight people on the *Mary Celeste* was a tragedy for them, their loved ones and their friends, there is one figure in the mystery who tends to be overlooked. Arthur Briggs was only seven years old when his parents and younger sister vanished without trace. Every day, he must have wondered what had happened. Arthur never found out. In the words of Captain Shufeldt, the fate of the *Mary Celeste* remains 'a sad and silent mystery of the sea'.

Göbekli Tepe

One of the most mysterious places on Earth, the complex of ancient stone circles known as Göbekli Tepe (meaning 'Potbelly Hill') inspires wonder and admiration in all those who come to see it. Built into a hillside near Sanliurfa in southern Turkey, this series of beautifully fashioned, crystalline limestone henges doesn't just keep its ancient secrets folded close to its chest – it's artistically dazzling, technologically brilliant and it is forcing us to rewrite the whole history of early human development.

Potbelly Hill's structures date from 9600–7300 BC, in the period known archaeologically as Pre-Pottery Neolithic A – 12,000 years ago. This is some *six thousand* years before the construction either of the Great Pyramid of Giza, or of Stonehenge. Its age and mystery ranks it as the least explained archaeological site of all time. According to long-and-dearly-held archaeological wisdom, it was only when we stopped being nomadic hunter-gatherers and settled down into farming communities that we had the steady food supplies, the time and the resources to develop complex societies, and spark the so-called 'knowledge revolution' that has culminated in the technological advances of modern life.

Göbekli Tepe turns all of this received conjecture on its head. The people who built this series of circular stone monuments had a mastery of engineering, art, architecture, mathematics and construction whose ingenuity would not be matched for more than five thousand years after the completion of its first phase. And yet what archaeological evidence there is suggests they were still semi-nomadic hunter-gatherers, and may only have occupied the site on special occasions. How is it that this group of people was so far in advance of the rest of the world, in almost every field of human endeavour, so far back in time?

Were they aliens, or given help by an extraterrestrial hand? That's one theory. The stones themselves are central to the mystery. Between 10 and 30 metres in diameter, each of the four major compounds excavated to date has a circular perimeter wall made of carefully cut, closely fitted blocks. The mere fact that they could work stone to this level of exactitude, almost matching but predating the Great Pyramid by thousands of years, is itself a pretty good advertisement for the builders' extraordinary skills. But it's the groups of monumental uprights placed at the centre of each henge that really set us back on our heels. Many of these look as if they are the idealised representations of superhuman figures: revered ancestors, gods, or some other entities we cannot explain. Twice the height of the shorter monoliths that surround them, but like them T-shaped, these giants stand more than six metres (20 feet) in height. Each upright weighs around 20 tonnes, immediately posing the same question as the one we are faced with at Stonehenge – how did the builders move and raise these enormous slabs?

Slender and elongated, the taller columns bear the faint, incised outlines of arms that terminate in hands with abnormally long fingers. These – like some of the Easter Island statues set up many thousands of years later – rest folded on the lower abdomen of what may – or may not – be meant to represent human figures. Some of the abstracted, eerie forms also wear necklaces, and what looks like a short cloak made of animal pelt – skinned from a wolf, perhaps, or a fox.

Most of the pillars are decorated with superbly executed

carvings of animals and insects: lions, snakes, spiders, scorpions, foxes and bulls. Executed both in three dimensions and as two-dimensional reliefs, the brilliance of these takes the breath away. Nothing like them had been seen since the best of the cave art produced by Neanderthals and early *Homo sapiens.* And nothing like them would be seen in art again for the best part of five thousand years. Even today, the level of skill on show in many of the carvings would be difficult to match. Different creatures dominate in each of the compounds, which may mean that each was built and/or used by a different clan or tribal group: the Scorpion People, the Fox Tribe, and so on.

Along with the crane or flamingo-like bird reliefs that decorate the surfaces of some of the monumental uprights, we find sinister, highly stylised vultures gazing as if at some distant prey. The carrion birds are clutching round objects that defy immediate explanation, but that may, according to experts, be the abstract representations of human heads.

Some archaeologists believe that these 'skull' images tell us that the people of Göbekli Tepe left their dead exposed to the elements, so that the vultures and crows could eat the remains, and then fly up into the air carrying the spirits of the dead to the heavens. In some of the more remote parts of central Asia, this form of 'sky burial' is still being practised today.

One of the many other strange things about Göbekli Tepe is that there is no evidence of long-term human occupation. Instead, as at Stonehenge, vast quantities of roughly butchered bones from seasonally hunted animals suggest the henges were used to hold epic meat-feasts: in celebration, for the purposes of ritual or worship, or simply for fun. The discovery of giant, 40-gallon stone troughs containing traces of calcium oxalate bear out that last notion: the chemical residue could very well be the result of the locals brewing the world's first beer. In which case, Göbekli Tepe may very well have been the venue for a seasonal jamboree – a bit like the UK's modern-day Glastonbury festival – or acted as a kind of prehistoric cultural and inter-tribal hub. If so, and if the theory that this group of extraordinary people had succeeded in arranging their lives so successfully that they had more fun and did less work than we do, then their technological know-how and environmental resourcefulness only adds to their mystery.

The picture that is emerging of a peaceful, settled community doing little work and devoting much of its time to pleasure has even led some commentators to suggest that Göbekli Tepe may be the origin of the biblical Garden of Eden, or of the paradise that features in some other religions – the folk-echo of a time when the majority of us didn't find ourselves screwed down by the relentless imperatives of money and work.

The site sits on the shoulder of a bald, rolling hill, one of many in the area that stretch for as far as the eye can see in every direction. While it is more or less barren now, it is believed that at the time the henges were built, the climate was gentler, with more rain, and that the landscape was greener, and home to rich and varied sources of game, including antelope.

Only four of the enigmatic stone structures have been fully excavated since their discovery by German archaeologist Klaus Schmidt in 1998. Geophysical surveys reveal that at least 16 other, similar megalithic complexes remain buried in the surrounding landscape, and Schmidt believed there may be dozens more. This means that, over the many hundreds of years between its various phases, there must have been thousands of people involved in the construction of Göbekli Tepe's numerous stone circles. This in turn tells us that they must have occupied the local area for extended, if intermittent, periods, and that when living there they must have had reliable food supplies.

Some experts now believe that, in order to supply the seasonal crowds who helped build and then celebrated or worshipped here, these same communities invented farming several thousand years earlier than was previously thought. Microscopic and DNA analysis of ancient cereal grains found nearby reveal they are the remains of the world's very first known varieties of wild einkorn and wild barley. This is the first ever known evidence of humans cultivating and cropping plants, and as with all the other 'firsts' that continue to stack up at Göbekli Tepe, wins the early farming race by a very long chalk.

What, then, was the real purpose of Göbekli Tepe? Did people come here to party, or to pray? Does the hilltop site mean it was an astronomical observatory, used to map the passage of the sun or the moon, or to foretell the impact of a comet? No one, as yet, can say for certain.

Instead of providing final answers, the more archaeologists examine the complex, the more the mystery of the Neolithic people who built it deepens. Some experts believe the stone circles may map out the very first zodiac. The ancient Babylonians have long been credited as the world's first astronomers. Yet Potbelly Hill suggests that this assumption, too, is wrong. Twelve stones mark the perimeter of Enclosure D – the magical twelve that marks the passage of our calendar months today, the same twelve we use on our clocks and in the zodiac. Why did its builders choose the base number twelve for their monumental architecture, when we have ten fingers and toes? And did their much earlier usage of the round dozen determine our own?

Scientists from the University of Edinburgh are working on a theory that the first circle built at Göbekli Tepe was a religious observatory, raised to mark, and perhaps foretell, the arrival of comets and meteor showers in Neolithic times. In this interpretation, the strange and exotic symbolism on one especially striking pillar, dubbed The Vulture Stone, documents the catastrophic impact of a comet that struck Earth around 11,000 BC.

If it did indeed smash into the Blue Planet – and experts differ as to whether or not the impact actually occurred – this devastating event would almost certainly have caused widespread environmental chaos. It may also have given rise to the mini Ice Age that scientists know as the 'Younger Dryas'. Evidence for the comet strike theory received a boost when researchers found a layer of super-tiny 'nanodiamonds' in the Younger Dryas geological layer. These tiny gemstones could only have been forged in conditions of extreme temperature and pressure, of the kind that occur when a comet strikes the Earth.

Does any of this hold water? The construction of the first compounds at Göbekli Tepe began in about 10,800 BC and ended circa 9600 BC – a time span that almost exactly matches the Younger Dryas event. Seen in this light, the strange symbolic pictogram on the Vulture Stone may not be a memorial that records excarnation, or a series of sky burials. It could instead be a direct reference both to the comet's impact, and to the environmental disaster that followed. The ball in the hand of the strange, beaked figure on the lower left quadrant of the relief is the comet; the vulture symbolises environmental mayhem.

One final unsolved mystery is the fact that at some point, the people of Göbekli Tepe abruptly abandoned the series of beautiful monuments they had worked so hard to create. Not only that, but in so far as the evidence currently shows, they deliberately buried them, and in so doing hid them from sight.

Why did they do this? Did they, for some obscure reason, want to hide the evidence of their prehistoric brilliance from future generations? Were they saddened by some setback, to the point where they literally wanted to bury the past? Or was it an act of archaeological altruism, designed to preserve this extraordinary legacy intact for future generations to discover and enjoy? Again, no one knows. One thing is for certain:

Göbekli Tepe is one of the most important prehistoric sites ever discovered. Wondrous and mysterious in themselves, the circles that have so far been excavated may only be the beginning of the greatest ever find in archaeological history.

The Great Pyramid of Giza

When it was new, the Great Pyramid must have seemed like a kind of surreal special effect, soaring up out of the khaki coloured desert-scape, dazzling onlookers and, in the brightest of sunlight, forcing them to look away. Wonder. Awe. Respect. These are the devices of a mighty ruler. And the person who commissioned the pyramid, as a funerary monument to himself, was the Fourth Dynasty Egyptian Pharaoh or 'god-king', Khufu, who had it built some 4,500 years ago.

Most of the pyramid we see today is missing the 170,000 tons of polished limestone facing that originally encased it, making the structure gleam a blinding, brilliant white in the sun – and ensuring it was visible from miles around in any direction. The few remaining slabs of this snowy outer cloak are so finely jointed that it is said to be impossible to slide the blade of a stiletto between them. Taken as a whole, the Great Pyramid represents a feat of engineering that, both now and even more so at the time, leaves us wondering: how did the Ancient Egyptians achieve it?

Sometimes, just when it seems as if science may have explained everything, demystifying an ancient wonder completely and for all time, the monument in question holds up a hand and says: 'Wait! I have more to reveal – but only if you know how to look.'

The Great Pyramid of Giza is one such defiant enigma,

throwing up new surprises and mysteries just when archaeologists – and the world's many avid pyramid watchers – least expect them.

The Great Pyramid has given up its secrets to generations of investigators only reluctantly, and bit by bit. They differ, often quite bitterly, about its significance; but they all agree on one thing: it is an astonishing monument, one of the most colossal single structures ever created, and one that has held its ancient secrets close to its chest. It may be about to unveil another.

The oldest of the Seven Wonders of the World, archaeologists believe that, in spite of its sheer size and internal complexity, the Great Pyramid was built in one mad dash, with a several-thousand-strong army of workers racing to complete it before Khufu's death, during a 10–20-year period that ended in around 2565 BC. (Experts disagree about the length of Khufu's reign – there is some consensus that it began in 2589 BC, but much less for how long it lasted, with estimates varying by as much as between 25 and 63 years.)

Khufu wanted his tomb to be the biggest and most impressive ever built, and in this he largely succeeded: soaring to a height of 147 metres (481.4 feet), the Great Pyramid remained the tallest and largest monument in the world for the best part of 4,000 years. Less fortunately, and if the idea was to keep Khufu's mummified remains safe for all eternity, the monument appears to have failed: despite the massive granite tomb at its heart, whose strange aura of power and superbly finished surfaces make it a fit resting-place for any monarch, not a single bone of Khufu's body has ever been found.

With a height of some 50 storeys, an estimated 2.3 million blocks of stone were used in the Great Pyramid's construction. Its 230-metre square footprint, with each 440-cubit/230.4-metre/756-foot side oriented exactly to the four points of the compass, covers an area roughly equivalent to six modern city blocks.

While it is one of the very few ways in which we can learn anything about him, the portrait of Khufu given to us by the Greek historian Herodotus is relentlessly damning. Writing in 440 BC, some 2,000 years after the pharaoh's death, and a further 2,500 years before our own time, Herodotus says: 'Down to the time when Rhampsinitos was king, they told me there was in Egypt nothing but orderly rule, and Egypt prospered greatly; but after him Cheops [as the Greeks later called Khufu] became king over them and brought them to every kind of evil. For he shut up all the temples, and having first kept them from sacrifices there, he then bade all the Egyptians work for him . . .' This suggests the pyramid was built on the back of mass national slavery – and yet, Herodotus tells us, Khufu still needed to raise a great deal of money for its construction.

Herodotus is often called 'the father of history' – but he might just as well be known as 'the father of malicious gossip'. He says that Khufu's cruelty and avarice were so great that he even forced one of his four female children into sex work to help raise the necessary funds for his mausoleum. The pharaoh's daughter, Herodotus tells us, duly set to work in the 'stews', but she had her own secret agenda: 'She not only obtained the sum appointed by her father, but also formed a private design to leave behind her a memorial, requesting each man who came in to give her one stone upon her building: and of these stones, they told me, the pyramid was built which stands in front of the great pyramid in the middle of the three.' A story that is almost certainly as inaccurate as it is salacious and designed at once to titillate readers, and diminish the earlier, competitor civilisation.

In fact, the three main pyramids at Giza were built and named for Khufu, Khafre and Menkaure respectively – all of them fourth dynasty kings, and with never a daughter in mind. They sit on the west bank of the River Nile in the district of Al-Jizah, from whence they take their anglicised name, a few short miles to the south and west of that sprawling modern-day Egyptian capital, Cairo.

The Great Pyramid has three secret chambers, the deepest of which was cut into the bedrock almost directly beneath its apex. All three chambers are near-vertically aligned. In some of the earlier pyramids, the lowermost chambers housed the pharaoh's tomb; but if the so-called 'Subterranean Chamber' beneath the Great Pyramid was ever intended for Khufu's remains, there was a change of plan. It was never finished. Instead, a previously concealed external entrance created 18 metres (59 feet) above ground in the structure's north face descends by means of a rough-hewn passage to open into a kind of man-made cavern carved from the bedrock. This has a small pit at its centre, whose purpose, like so much else about the Great Pyramid, is unknown. From this cramped and claustrophobic space, a new tunnel runs on a short distance, only to culminate in an abrupt dead-end – again as if the builders – or more likely, Khufu – had experienced a change of heart.

Going back to the Descending Passage, it seems to have been more than 3,000 years before anyone discovered the existence of a new passageway angling steeply up from a point some 30 metres along its length. One story goes that it only came to light in the early ninth century AD, when the Abbasid caliph Ma'mun (AD 813–833) had a team of workers dig a speculative tunnel into the pyramid's north face. They attacked the structure at ground level below what we now know was the previously concealed entrance to the Descending Passage. As luck would have it – and in this case, Ma'mun (or Al-Mamun) and his men were spectacularly lucky – their tunnel struck into the Descending Passage at the precise point where a mighty granite slab, whose whole purpose had been to conceal the entrance to the Ascending Passage, had been wedged and then camouflaged with limestone facing to look like the surrounding structural blocks.

Too good to be true, and, in terms of the diggers just happening to strike in at the right spot – too much of a coincidence to be true? We only know about Ma'mun's expedition from accounts written hundreds of years later, and not at the time, so the jury is out both on their accuracy and on the tale as a whole.

None of this takes away from the majesty and mystery of the Great Pyramid, nor from what Ma'mun's men reportedly discovered next. The Ascending Passage spears on up into the heart of the pyramid, before suddenly opening out onto a breathtaking, 8.5-metre-high 'Grand Gallery'. Formed of massive, precision-jointed granite blocks, the Grand Gallery acts as a magnificent ceremonial avenue that culminates in the equally extraordinary, tomb-like space known as the King's Chamber. This contains the massive red granite sarcophagus apparently intended for Khufu's remains. The only problem being that not so much as a pharaonic finger bone has ever been found in it. There is also no trace or record whatsoever that any of the gold or precious artefacts or the grave goods we see in other ancient royal Egyptian burials were discovered in the chamber. The whole space remains eerily – and inexplicably – empty.

Five compact vertical chambers are ranged vertically above the King's Chamber, with an inverted 'V'-shaped weight-relieving capstone placed on top of them. A narrow crawl space leading from the top end of the Grand Gallery ends in a final and once-secret chamber. This was only discovered when someone dynamited the heavy slab of stone that had been blocking access to it. The walls of the strange little room beyond are covered in graffiti scrawled on its walls in the nineteenth century.

But there is one remaining Ancient Egyptian message. Picked out in a series of small red cartouches, it reads: 'Khufu's Gang was here.'

A narrower, horizontal passageway leads from the base of the Grand Gallery to the Queen's Chamber. So-called 'air shafts' lead from both the Queen's and the King's Chambers to the pyramid's exterior. The pair leading from the Queen's Chamber end in mysterious little 'doors' – but as the shafts were investigated by means of a robot, no one knows what, if anything, lies on the other side. Do they conceal the entrance to the real tombs, containing the mummified bodies of King Khufu and his Queen and twin hoards of fabulous treasure? Is the King's Chamber, the Grand Gallery and the whole system of passageways discovered to date nothing more than an elaborate blind, constructed to conceal the as yet hidden truth? We can only speculate – and hope.

Most Egyptians, in the time of Khufu, believed that the pharaoh's body must be preserved in order to ensure not just his majestic prosperity in the afterlife, but their own continued survival. In both life and death, the health of the pharaoh and the society he ruled were therefore viewed as one and the same thing. Each, in this mystical symbiosis, needed the other to survive. Much of this belief centred on the behaviour of the River Nile: when the pharaoh was in good health and pleased, then by dint of what we would think of as sympathetic magic, the Nile would deliver its annual bounty – the optimal volume of water that irrigated the land, ensuring its fertility and sufficient food crops for the year.

There was more: once he had successfully taken up his heavenly residence with Ra, the pharaoh could whisper the wishes of the people into the Sun God's ear. The only snag being that, in order to ensure a successful afterlife, Khufu's tomb had to be ready to receive his remains *before* he died. A post-mortem mausoleum would be too late. Which is why the second pharaoh of the Fourth Dynasty of the Old Kingdom of Egypt engaged thousands of skilled and unskilled labourers, working against – and very likely right round – the clock to complete it in time. Six million tons of stone had to be quarried, hauled to the site, measured, cut and dressed exactly to size and shape and then placed with previously unparalleled accuracy to create the structure. This again suggests the workforce was not made up of slaves, dragooned by the evil Khufu, but of willing employees, paid either in money, food and accommodation, or all of the above.

The fact that the builders achieved their royal mission in the space of some 25 years, using nothing more than copper, stone and wooden tools, is a marvel in its own right. What really challenges belief, though, is that if the estimate of 2.3 million blocks used in the Great Pyramid's construction is correct, it means that a workforce of between 20,000 and 30,000 labourers must have placed one of the great blocks, each weighing an average of two tonnes, into position every six minutes, 24 hours a day, seven days a week, for 25 years. In the baking heat, and in the teeth of sandstorms, the occasional downpour, and, almost certainly, outbreaks of disease. How, given among other things the obvious difficulty of working at night, was this practically possible?

The Pyramid Scrolls

In 2013, a French architect made a truly remarkable find. Hidden in a sealed cache 150 miles away from Giza at a place named Wadi Al-Jarf, on the eastern side of the Red Sea, Pierre Tallet discovered the world's oldest known rolls of papyrus. One of the long-buried documents turned out to be the diary of an overseer named Merer. In the 26th year of Khufu's reign, in 2563 BC, Merer was in charge of a 200-strong crew – one of many such named and competing teams of men – that was tasked with moving stones for the Great Pyramid. Merer tells us that he and his men routinely stopped at Tura, some eight miles from Giza, to pick up the high-quality limestone blocks for which the quarry was famous. They then manhandled them on to purpose-built boats, and shipped them on to the construction site.

Since the Ancient Egyptians thought it was impossible to move hundreds of multi-ton blocks of stone 150 miles overland – something that is worth considering in the context of Stonehenge – archaeologists are now convinced that along with everything else, Khufu ordered the construction of a new canal system. This stupendous feat of engineering ended in a dock right next door to the pyramid. Nearby, Khufu ordered the construction of the world's first, two-storey apartment blocks to house his army of workers; fed them by producing bread on a truly industrial scale, and in the process triggered a huge increase in Egyptian farming.

Khufu's monumental innovations also meant building an extensive network of transport links, including a jetty near Wadi Al-Jarf to serve the world's first large-scale artificial harbour. Precious copper was shipped in from Sinai to fashion the chisels used in cutting the stones; wood came from Lebanon; turquoise perhaps from Afghanistan; while the granite used to create the Grand Gallery and the tomb was transported up the Nile from Aswan.

Did Khufu bankrupt Ancient Egypt with all of this frenzied activity? Did people starve, as workers were siphoned away from their farms and garden plots to work on the new infrastructure? Not a bit of it. As a result of all of his ingenuity – which includes the establishment of a monumental bureaucracy

– this remarkable ruler kick-started the world's first large-scale industrial economy, building not just his own mausoleum, but arguably laying the foundations of what has become modern Egypt.

How, in the space of less than 200 years, did the Ancient Egyptians go from building the unsophisticated mud-brick 'step' pyramids known as *mastabas* (Arabic 'benches') like the one King Zoser had built at Saqqara in 2750 BC, to the highly complex, monumental stone architecture of the Great Pyramid? The interval doesn't quite seem long enough for such a quantum technological or imaginative leap. This is why there are some who believe the pyramid's builders must have had a helping hand. One striking if unsubstantiated idea is that ancient mentors, or 'Old Ones', the proof of whose presence and superior knowledge is now, the theorists maintain, largely lost to us, helped Khufu complete the work.

Sticking to less fanciful explanations, it may be that one of the reasons for the great architectural leap forward was a better understanding of mathematics. The Great Pyramid is designed in the form of a four-sided equilateral triangle, with a uniform incline of 51.8 degrees. That angle is determined by the ratio of the pyramid's height to the radius of the circle whose circumference exactly encloses the square plan of the base. Now, that's clever.

How did the pyramid's builders manage to cut the angled stones used on its facing so precisely, especially as they were working at such speed? Again, the answer lies in a brilliant use of mathematics. Using geometry and trigonometry, the builders worked out that they need only take two measurements: a horizontal measure of 14 units, and a vertical measure of 11 units, to ensure that all the stones were angled in exactly the same way, giving the pyramid a perfect uniform slope of a smidgen less than 52 degrees. Which, by way of comparison, is a good

15 or so degrees steeper than the landing slope of the average modern ski-jump.

Once they'd fashioned them, how did they get all the blocks into position? Herodotus has something to say on this subject, too:

> This pyramid was made after the manner of steps which some called 'rows' and others 'bases': and when they had first made it thus, they raised the remaining stones with machines made of short pieces of timber. They began by raising them from the ground to the first stage of the steps, and when the stone got up to this it was placed upon another machine standing on the first stage. So from there it was drawn to the second upon another machine; for as many as were the courses of the steps, so many machines there were also; or perhaps they transferred one and the same machine, made so as easily to be carried, to each stage successively, in order that they might take up the stones; for let it be told in both ways, according as it is reported.
>
> However that may be, the highest parts of the pyramid were finished first, and afterwards they proceeded to finish that which came next to them, and lastly they finished the parts of it near the ground and the lowest ranges.

If that sounds confusing, that's because it is. How, if its builders 'began at the base', were 'the highest parts of the pyramid finished first'?

Some researchers believe the finished blocks were moved up a specially constructed ramp from the dock to the emerging pyramid using a system of wooden sledges, rollers, ropes and rails – and a lot of human muscle power. It may very well have been that if they really did actually use them, the Ancient Egyptians greased the sledges and rails with animal fat. Something that might equally well have been the case at Stonehenge. Others argue that a ramp of the necessary size and shape would have taken more effort and longer to build than the pyramid itself, thereby ruling it out. One recent and ingenious solution to this particular conundrum is the idea that, while the pyramid's outer shell was formed of carefully cut blocks, its interior was filled with the offcuts and rubble left over from that same shaping. Unless Khufu had it all transported elsewhere, again at the cost of enormous time and effort, this account of its construction might also explain why there isn't a gigantic pile of stone waste near the Great Pyramid.

Aiming for the Stars

Given the enormous size and weight of the granite slabs that were used to create the pharaoh's tomb and its ceremonial passageway, it's tempting to speculate that the builders *began* with these structures, and then built the rest of the pyramid around them. If not, can we believe that, having completed the gigantic, solid stone structure as a whole, they then carved the access passageways, the Grand Gallery and the tomb itself by hand from its interior; somehow manoeuvred the giant granite blocks up and into place, and then constructed the finished funerary complex from the inside out? One pyramid, so many puzzles.

Some commentators believe that the alignment of the three main pyramids directly and deliberately replicates the alignment of certain stars, either as they were disposed in the heavens at the time of the pyramid's construction, or even earlier. In this theory, the Giza pyramids are configured not just in such a way as to help the pharaohs ascend to their divine calling, but to act as a kind of giant astronomical alarm clock. This supposedly provides a record of past disasters that have befallen Earth – for example, the last Ice Age – and warns of future catastrophes, but again, we are in the realms of speculation.

What's not in doubt is that the two slim 'air-shafts' that radiate diagonally upwards from the King's Chamber pierce the pyramid's outer skin and seem to take aim at the heavens. The southern shaft is thought by some to align directly with Alnilam, the middle star of Orion's belt. This supposedly identifies Alnilam with Osiris, the Egyptian god of death, resurrection and fertility. The northern shaft is said to target 'the Dragon' constellation, Alpha Draconis.

The 'Orion correlation theory' proposes that all three of the larger Giza pyramids correlate with Alnitak, Alnilam and Mintaka, the three stars that make up Orion's belt. In this way of looking at things, the Sphinx then represents the constellation of Leo, while the River Nile corresponds to the Milky Way. While they are intriguing, the validity of these alignment claims is hotly disputed, with many Egyptologists and scientists rebutting them outright.

Other theories about the Great Pyramid's significance abound. Some 'pyramidologists' speculate that it encodes predictions for major historical events. These include the Exodus of Moses from Egypt, the crucifixion of Jesus Christ and the outbreak of the First World War. By measuring what they call 'pyramid inches,' to calculate the passage of time, the Giza pyramid also supposedly warns of a forthcoming Armageddon. In this scheme of reckoning, one British inch is equal to one solar year.

The complete absence of Khufu's remains has led some to speculate that the Great Pyramid was never in reality meant for him, but as a cosmic energy accumulator, or as a kind of repository for ancient wisdom.

*

Until recently, many thought that less than one-tenth of one per cent of the pyramid's interior was open space, while the remaining 99.9-odd per cent was solid rock. Whatever the truth, late in 2017, Dr Kunihiro Morishima and his colleagues from Nagoya University, Japan, announced that they had discovered a new and previously unknown void lying at the heart of the Great Pyramid that is many times bigger than Khufu's tomb. If it proves to be true then it is a stunning discovery.

The research team used a groundbreaking scientific technique known as cosmic-ray muon radiography to investigate the pyramid's internal structure non-invasively. Muons – subatomic particles that are a by-product of cosmic rays – are only partially absorbed by solid stone. This means they can be used to create what is essentially an X-ray image of stone structures. Applied to the Great Pyramid, the team reports the imaging came up with an extraordinary result: the existence of a large empty space directly above the Grand Gallery.

At least 30 metres (98 feet) long, the cross-section of the void is similar in volume to that of the Grand Gallery below, and according to the early scans runs roughly parallel to it. No one as yet knows what, if anything, lies within; it is not yet entirely certain if the space is horizontal, or angled; and no one can say why it was created. Is it simply a 'relieving chamber' to save weight? Or will it turn out to have some other, much more thrilling purpose? The 'ScanPyramids' project, as it is known, also claims to have discovered a second, smaller, corridor-shaped cavity behind the pyramid's north face.

Renowned Egyptologist, archaeologist and Egypt's former Minister of Antiquities Affairs, Dr Zahi Hawass is one of the world's leading experts on the Great Pyramid. Hawass dismisses excitement over the voids. He said that having met with some of the project's scientists and reviewed their conclusions, he informed them that, 'There is no new discovery.'

Dr Morishima counters that the cavity 'was not known by anyone until now, from when the pyramid was built 4,500 years ago'. He said 'the big void is completely closed', and anything inside it would not therefore have been 'touched by anyone since the pyramid was built'.

Whoever turns out to be in the right, with the advent of increasingly sophisticated techniques such as muon imaging and Light Detection and Ranging (LIDAR), science is shedding new light on ancient structures.

No invasive drilling is generally allowed by the Egyptian authorities into the pyramid's heart, but it may be that they will permit a tiny, deflated airship to be inserted through a 1.5-inch (3.8cm) hole punched into the smaller 'corridor void', always assuming it exists. Once inside, the airborne scout will be inflated and flown around the space while its onboard camera takes and records pictures. The flying robot will then be deflated and extracted through the same borehole, and its evidence examined. Will it find treasure or 'wonderful things'? Or will it just turn out to be a lot of hot air? We may be on the verge of some great new discovery – but it's hard not to believe that, given the choice, King Khufu would much rather the pyramid's essential mystery remained intact.

Stonehenge

Let's take a trip back into the late Neolithic and zoom in on the period around 2500 BC, when stone in all its forms enjoyed mystical significance not just in Britain, or Europe, but across the globe. Nowhere is this more apparent than at Stonehenge, the world-famous monument erected on Salisbury Plain, a 300-square-mile (780km²) stretch of sparsely populated land in west-central southern England. Home to the endangered Adonis blue butterfly, *Polyommatus bellargus*, it also plays host to a slew of rare British plants that include the burnt-tip orchid (*Neotinea ustulata*), bastard toadflax (*Thesium humifusum*), squinancy-wort (*Asperula cynanchica*), slender bedstraw (*Gallium pumilum*) and the delicious-sounding Devil's-bit scabious (*Succisa pratensis*). The British military currently uses about half the area for training, and the lack of public access to the landscape helps keep struggling species alive.

Even today, then, the plain is a singular and special place. What must it have been like 4,500 years ago, when a large community of diverse people decided to make it even more significant? And why choose this open and featureless patch of rolling chalk downland in particular? Does the answer, as some experts believe, lie in the fact that two of the largest monoliths, including the one we know as the Heel Stone, were already lying in place, left there by a retreating glacier at the end of the last Ice Age? The idea makes a lot of sense, but has yet to be proven.

Recent evidence strongly suggests the smaller stones that make up Stonehenge, known as 'bluestones', were quarried and then moved from rock outcrops at Craig Rhos-y-felin and Carn Goedog, in Pembrokeshire, west Wales. On average, the naturally occurring pillars – which archaeologists believe the monument's builders split from the rock using wooden wedges swelled by the action of Welsh rain – weigh a couple of tonnes. As much as a family car, only unlike a car, they don't have wheels. And they come in big, ungainly lumps. So moving them over any kind of distance is extremely difficult. Yet the people who built Stonehenge somehow managed to transport several dozen of these rocky brutes more than 140 miles from the north side of the Preseli hills to Salisbury Plain, and then arrange them in patterns that were special to them, but to us remain mysterious.

How did they do it? Some believe the boulders were loaded onto wooden pallets, which teams of people simply carried. Another idea is that they were dragged by oxen/human power on sledges and/or rollers greased with animal fat. In this scenario, they were heaved up and down the intervening hills to present-day Milford Haven, shipped from there to modern Bristol by sea, and then rafted down the inland river networks to Stonehenge. Would you like to try shipping a four- or five-ton boulder up the Bristol Channel on an elementary wooden boat; decant it onto a raft and hope that, somehow, neither of these craft would sink en route; and then, when you have finally got it to the banks of the River Avon near Stonehenge, manhandle it up to the building site?

No traces of ancient boats from the first construction period have ever been found at any of the likely sites, but then being wooden, they would only have survived if they had been preserved in something like peat. Yet these craft, if they existed, must have been pretty big and solid to freight all that weight and remain stable – and the same must have been true of any rafts. Unless the boat-builders had discovered the trick of using ballast to aid stability, then even in calm waters the risk of capsize must have been great. Given this, it seems more likely that the monoliths were moved overland for the entire distance. Yet this represents the most mammoth amount of effort and skill, and must have involved dozens – if not hundreds – of people working in relays for months – if not years – on end.

The recent chemical matching of Stonehenge bluestones to the Craig Rhos-y-felin and Carn Goedog outcrops does, though, at least seem to rule out the theory that these particular stones were deposited near Stonehenge by a glacier during the last Ice Age.

The monument whose extraordinary remains we see today started life around 3000 BC as a circular ditch and bank earthwork with an internal diameter of 85 metres pierced by twin entrances: one about ten metres wide to the north-east, and a smaller, five metre-wide entrance to the south. At the same time, a series of 56 pits known as 'Aubrey Holes' (after John Aubrey, the antiquarian and scholar who first noticed them in 1666) was dug around the internal perimeter of this proto-henge. Many of these pits contained cremation remains, and there is evidence of more cremation burials in the bottom of the ditch, mostly on the eastern side.

Nobody agrees about much at Stonehenge, least of all the experts; but it is generally believed that, beginning in 2900 BC, the first stones to be set up inside this original ditch and bank henge were the bluestones, again suggesting their overall importance in the scheme. Twin concentric rows of about 40 bluestones each were placed in a double horseshoe shape, with the open end of the arrangement facing south-west. At the same time the first of the even bigger sarsen stones, known as the Altar Stone, was set up at a point where the bluestone horseshoe, if it had been continued to form an oval, would have conjoined.

(A sarsen is a sandstone block, and unlike the bluestones, there are many of them lying on the surface near Stonehenge, both on Salisbury Plain and on the Marlborough Downs.)

Four more sarsen monoliths known as the Station Stones were then placed in a neat rectangle some five metres in from the henge perimeter. These stones appear to align with the midsummer sunrise, the midwinter sunset and the major northern moonset.

If people moved the bluestones all the way from west Wales, then – leaving aside the puzzle of how – the even bigger question is *why* did they seek to move them in the first place? Why these monoliths, in particular, over stretches of terrain that made the task of transporting them especially difficult? Why were the Welsh bluestones so important that ancient Britons valued them above all others?

One theory is that the bluestones were believed to have healing powers, especially when anointed with water. If true, then this would make Stonehenge a kind of giant, mystical healing centre, where people from all points of the compass came to seek cures. Others point to the musical properties of the bluestones – it is said that when struck in a certain way, they give off a loud, ringing note, a bit like a modern church bell, that might have been used to summon people to the site for the purposes of ritual, community discussion or celebration.

Was an earlier, intermediary henge made of these very same bluestones erected somewhere between Wales and Stonehenge? A lost monument which was subsequently dismantled, and from which they were taken and reused? This would at least mean that the megaliths were moved in two stages, and not in one dauntingly long haul.

Did the people who built Stonehenge believe that by moving them, they somehow animated a spirit within the stones? One that in some way invested them with magical power? That would still beg the question, why those particular stones? Like so much else concerning this global icon, there are plenty of questions, but not very many people agree on the answers.

What we do know is that Stonehenge didn't suddenly appear, or rise up fully formed in the space of a generation or two like the Great Pyramid. Rather, it was built within a much wider and much older ritual landscape – one that is rich in other stone and wooden structures, processional ways and round and long barrows, not to mention dozens of ancient burial sites and many sizeable and carefully constructed enclosures.

Several pits, three of which held large wooden 'totem poles', were dug near Stonehenge between 8500 and 7000 BC, long before the actual stone structures were begun, but no one is sure whether these early traces have a direct connection with the later monument. Hundreds of animal bone and flint fragments tell us that, during that same early period, ancient hunters lived very close to the spot where Stonehenge was finally constructed, and not far from Blick Mead, a reliable fresh water spring nearby. The eventual site of the henge may, then, have been on an aurochs migration route – your aurochs (it always has an 's' at the end) being a type of huge, ferocious bull that could feed up to 200 people, and that even Julius Caesar tells us he treated with due respect.

The Blick Mead spring is a very strange and rather special place in its own right. The pool it feeds is home to a singular species of algae that grows on the pebbles and rocks. When exposed to the air, the algae turns spectacular shades of bright, reddish-pink. This startling phenomenon, which must have seemed magical to pre-scientific eyes, may very well have helped people decide the location merited ritual, celebration, and the erection of a fitting tribute in stone.

The wider Stonehenge area then evolved continuously over the next several thousand years, beginning with the bank and ditch earthworks we've already mentioned, and wooden structures. By 3500 BC, the Greater, or Stonehenge, Cursus and the Lesser Cursus had been created. These gigantic, elongated earthworks, which may have been processional ways, lie respectively just to the north and north-west of Stonehenge itself. (One early commentator thought that the Greater Cursus might have been an early racecourse . . .) A further vast, causewayed enclosure at a site known as Robin Hood's Ball was also created nearby. Whether these earlier monuments influenced the location of Stonehenge proper is also unknown, but seems likely.

Around 2500 BC, evidence suggests that Stonehenge was reconfigured, again for reasons unknown: the bluestones were moved from their original positions in the henge, and work began on the huge Sarsen Circle. Imagine setting up 30 four-metre rocky monoliths, each weighing between 6 and 50 tons, and then arranging them in a ring measuring 30 metres in diameter. And you have to do it without metal tools, electricity, or any of the useful modern machinery, such as a crane, that we take for granted. Somehow, the builders managed the task, and then placed six-ton lintel stones on top of the uprights using the mortise and tenon joints we still see used in carpentry today. These formed a continuous stone cap or architrave around the circle, some of which is now sadly missing. Modern conservationist doctrine prevents any alteration to the stones, but wouldn't it be great to see the circle once again complete and in all its glory?

Five absolutely gigantic sarsen trilithons were then erected inside the great sarsen circle, which you could say acts as a kind of frame or setting for them. Like the original bluestones, the trilithons were initial positioned in a horseshoe configuration. This time, though, the open end of the horseshoe faced north-east, towards a new entrance.

The largest, or 'Great Trilithon' set up in the south-west quadrant towers a massive 7.3 metres (24ft) tall. The heaviest of the stones used at Stonehenge, its twin uprights weigh a mind-boggling 50 tons apiece. Archaeologists believe these huge sarsens were brought from an area of the Marlborough Downs 20 miles (32km) or so to the north. Even though they didn't have to come as far as the bluestones, transporting these enormous lumps of stone must have posed a different order of difficulty again for the many hundreds of people who presumably moved them.

The bluestones were repositioned at various times, until they ended up in the configuration we see today.

The processional way now known as The Avenue was also built during the final building phase, connecting Stonehenge with the River Avon a little over a mile to the south-east. Like elements of the henge, including the famous Heel Stone 20 metres from the north-east entrance, the final 500 metres of The Avenue aligns with the axis of the midsummer sunrise. It leads celebrants or ritual worshippers – if that's what the site was used for – up to and into the henge.

One of the many other unanswered questions we have to ask about Stonehenge is: why did people come here from places far from the British Isles? For come they most certainly did. One of them was a boy found buried on nearby Boscombe Down. The DNA of this young man, who was about fourteen when he died in 1550 BC, reveals that he was born somewhere in the Mediterranean, in southern France or Spain, or even, some experts believe, as far away as modern Greece. Other human remains suggest a strong link with people from modern-day Wales, which is perhaps not so surprising when we remember that the bluestones came from what is now the Pembrokeshire Coast National Park.

The grave of the man known as the 'Amesbury Archer', who

lived around 2300 BC, was discovered two miles from Stonehenge in 2002. His body and the grave goods found with it were carefully arranged in a wooden chamber that was purpose-built for him and then covered by a low earth mound. Viewed as one of the most important European archaeological discoveries, the grave contained more than 100 items, far more than any other burial from this time. Among the many riches brought to light were eighteen arrowheads and two archer's wrist guards, four boar's tusks, 122 flint tools, a metalworking kit that included a cushion stone, and three copper knives. The knives may have been samples of this man's seemingly magical new ability to smelt and work metal, which he displayed to gain new business. The beautiful hair ornaments also uncovered in the burial are the oldest gold objects ever to be found in Britain. Visit the Salisbury museum, and you can see the contents of this wonderful find for yourself.

Tests on the Archer's teeth show he was born outside the British Isles, somewhere in the Alps and most likely in modern-day Switzerland. His left kneecap was missing, which would have caused him to limp, and he had a hole in his jaw caused by what must have been an extremely painful dental abscess. The Archer's son – or a very close relation – who had also travelled from the same Alpine region was buried beside him. Metalworkers enjoyed special status as the Bronze Age gradually overtook the age of stone, which may explain the extraordinary care taken in the Archer's burial.

Death and funerary memorials in general seems to have played an important role in the development of Stonehenge. There are dozens of burial sites in the surrounding landscape, including one discovered in 2017 beneath a wheat field between Stonehenge and Avebury. Labelled 'The House of the Dead', and dating from 3700–3500 BC, experts believe that this new find, which is still being investigated, was a mass necropolis.

A prehistoric village discovered at nearby Durrington Walls may have housed its builders during key construction phases of Stonehenge. Evidence of seasonal feasting on meat and dairy products at the Durrington site suggests the many generations of people who built the henge and associated monuments were not enslaved. Perhaps they worked voluntarily or in return for their keep. More romantically, it may be that they were fired by the collective idea of raising a spiritual totem that would stand for thousands of years as a tribute to their culture and beliefs. A giant stone henge that lasts for many millennia is not, after all, such a bad way of marking your existence. Whatever the truth of it, whoever first persuaded people it was a good idea to build a massive circular stone monument with the primitive technology available at the time possessed unique charismatic and persuasive power. The various iterations of Stonehenge took hundreds of years to complete, entailing successive generations in backbreaking work. Building the monument must, though, have been a task that brought people of all ages and from different regions of the British Isles together in a common purpose. If you were looking to unify disparate tribes and groups from all corners of a country, then a collective effort like the building of Stonehenge must have been a wonderful way of achieving that.

Let's join Tess Durbeyfield/d'Urberville and Angel Clare, the two lead characters from local author Thomas Hardy's 1891 novel *Tess of the d'Urbervilles*, as in its closing pages it describes their fictional encounter with Stonehenge. Fleeing from the authorities in the deep of night, after Tess has murdered Alec, the man who raped her, Tess and Angel stumble into an unknown but massive structure:

> He listened. The wind, playing upon the edifice, produced a booming tune, like the note of some gigantic one-stringed harp.

No other sound came from it, and lifting his hand and advancing a step or two, Clare felt the vertical surface of the structure. It seemed to be of solid stone, without joint or moulding. Carrying his fingers onward he found that what he had come in contact with was a colossal rectangular pillar; by stretching out his left hand he could feel a similar one adjoining. At an indefinite height overhead something made the black sky blacker, which had the semblance of a vast architrave uniting the pillars horizontally. They carefully entered beneath and between; the surfaces echoed their soft rustle; but they seemed to be still out of doors. The place was roofless. Tess drew her breath fearfully, and Angel, perplexed, said –

'What can it be?'

Feeling sideways they encountered another tower-like pillar, square and uncompromising as the first; beyond it another and another. The place was all doors and pillars, some connected above by continuous architraves.

'A very Temple of the Winds,' he said.

And for all that we know, of the sun, and the moon, and the stars. Celestial observatory? Neolithic party venue? Giant necropolis? Healing clinic? European cultural exchange and business hub? We cannot reduce the wonder of this extraordinary monument to easy interpretations. For as long as it stands, like Angel Clare and Tess of the d'Urbervilles, people will go on trying to unravel its mysteries.

Teotihuacan

It's a scene that might have come straight from an Indiana Jones movie. Studying the ancient Mesoamerican city of Teotihuacan in 2003, Mexican archaeologist Sergio Gómez Chávez came across a sinkhole. Newly opened following days of heavy rain, it lay at the base of the Temple of the Feathered Serpent, the third largest pyramid in the complex. Worried it might swallow some of the thousands of tourists who visit the site every year, Chávez shone a torch down the hole. The light yawned away into Stygian darkness. Intrigued, he got some workmen to lower him down on a rope. Once inside, he was very surprised, like Alice in Wonderland, to discover the shaft went down and down to a depth much greater than he could have anticipated. Not only that, it was perfectly circular, and it also appeared to have been dug by hand. Then, at a certain point in his descent, a horrible stink came up from the void – one that threatened to make him gag. Trying to ignore the overpowering stench, he carried on. When he reached the bottom 14 metres down, Chávez stood in wonder, half-expecting to meet some strange, benighted creature from the realms of fiction: a Mexican Mad Hatter, perhaps, or a grinning Ciudad Apodaca cat.

Instead, raising the torch, he discovered the shaft opened out onto even greater wonders. A second, horizontal passageway that was also perfectly cylindrical ran away in both directions from where he was standing. Two enormous boulders, that had obviously been placed there on purpose, blocked this corridor to either side. Chávez called up for his colleagues to hoist him back up. He was going to need their help to shift the boulders – but it looked as if the effort might repay them a thousand fold. Judging by what he had already seen, the main stretch of tunnel behind one of the rock plugs ran roughly 100 metres, linking the Ciudadela to the Temple of the Plumed Serpent. If that were true, and if the ancient citizens of this fabled city had put the giant obstructions there to deter robbers, then his worldwide reputation as an archaeologist was made.

Chávez hardly dared to watch as a new team got busy clearing the way. The work seemed to proceed with excruciating slowness. At last, the call he had been waiting for sounded up the shaft: 'We've moved it. You can go in.' Feeling even more like a real-life Indiana Jones, Chávez led the way inside. His initial estimation proved right: the tunnel speared directly beneath the great central plaza of Teotihuacan. Almost exactly 100 metres long, it ended in an amazing discovery: three rock-cut chambers filled with riches. He had stumbled on one of the most important archaeological finds in modern history.

One of the most visited, most impressive and most intriguing sites in the world, the ancient city of Teotihuacan lies some 40 kilometres (25 miles) north-east of Mexico City. With a total surface area of 83 square kilometres (32 sq. miles), the city and its estimated 125,000 people flourished for approximately 800 years between 100 BC and AD 700–800 – but no one is sure exactly when or why this sophisticated metropolis collapsed.

The name 'Teotihuacan' most likely translates as 'birthplace of the gods'. Predating Aztec civilisation by almost 700 years, from its early beginnings on an area of marshy land it grew to incorporate thousands of residential compounds and ceremonial buildings. Some of these, in the style of modern day apartment blocks, are multi-storey.

In the more upscale of the surviving dwellings, the walls were adorned with brilliant murals such as the somewhat daunting image of the Great Goddess. She may very well have been the city-state's primary deity.

Astonishing, impressive ceremonial architecture towers over a broad central thoroughfare known as 'The Avenue of the Dead'. Aligned on a north–south axis in concert with the other monuments, this links the Temple of the Sun with the Ciudad-ela, or courtyard of the Plumed Serpent. Astonishing to report, the city's majestic stone pyramids and platforms were originally painted in shades of dark maroon and blood red. They include the Pyramid of the Moon, the Pyramid of the Sun, and the Temple of the Feathered Serpent, or Quetzalcoatl. There is also a huge market place, and many lesser religious and ritual sites. The great sacred 'Fat Mountain', Cerro Gordo, looms in the background over all.

Spooling back to the tunnel discovery, four greenstone stat-ues stand out among the objects Chávez and his team brought to light. Like mini, idealised humans – perhaps priests – they have bright, shining crystalline eyes, and clothing carved into their forms. Exploring further in this chamber of wonders, Chávez found large numbers of pyrite mirrors, seashells that must have held some special significance and dozens of sym-bolic pendants. It is thought that priests or shamans may have used these in arcane rituals, in an effort to communicate with other realms.

In total, more than 74,000 items were recovered from the subterranean complex. They included marvellous sculptures of jaguars, a box of carefully arranged beetle wings, more humanoid figurines, all manner of jade and terracotta objects, ceramics, jewellery and animal bones. Dozens of superbly fashioned obsidian artefacts also saw the light of day for the first time in the best part of two thousand years: striking masks, whose purpose is uncertain but which may have had some kind of funerary function; ornamental items that may have been traded with neighbouring settlements; tools, and many other items.

No less mysterious is the model landscape – like an ancient diorama – that was also discovered in the tunnel. Complete with miniature, hand-sculpted mountains and little pools of liquid mercury that seem to have represented 'lakes', this model and the corridor in which it stands are thought to mirror the underworld, the lowest of the three levels: celestial, earthly and subterranean, in which the citizens of Teotihuacan – like so many other people over the millennia – believed. Unlike the fiery and destructive Christian hell, though, Teotihuacan's underground aquatic realm was a place of creation and rebirth.

To make their illusory underworld even more convincing, its builders impregnated the tunnel's ceiling with a glittering powder composed of pyrite, haematite and magnetite. When it was bright and new, this stardust must have made people feel as if they were standing under the very vault of heaven, with the planets and stars strung out across the sky overhead.

The whole elaborate installation – tunnel, diorama and all – comes across as a place of ritual, where citizens could discover and reconfirm their founding creation myths, and leave offerings to appease Teotihuacan's fearsome gods – not least the fanged and bloodthirsty Storm God, whose bulging eyes missed nothing, and who could rain down lightning, fire and destruction if in any way displeased.

Not everything about Teotihuacan leaves us gazing in admiration. In an effort to keep the gods on their side and to ensure the city's prosperity, its people practised human sacrifice. Hundreds of victims – believed the most part to be captured male enemy warriors – were variously buried alive, decapitated, had their hearts cut out, or were bludgeoned to death. There is also evidence that many animals, including mountain lions, wolves, eagles and venomous snakes were ritually sacrificed.

For all of this routine horror, the beauty, strangeness and outstanding craftsmanship of the artefacts discovered in the ruins of Teotihuacan continue to thrill and amaze art historians, archaeologists and the public alike. Thousands of objects have been painstakingly unearthed, cleaned and meticulously catalogued. And yet we still don't yet know as much as we would like to about the origins, expansion, reach and demise of this extraordinary civilisation. Who built it? How did they become so accomplished in the management of complex stone architecture? Who burned and smashed the city sometime around AD 750, and why?

Hundreds of clay balls encased in a shiny, metallic shell of yellow jarosite ('fool's gold', or oxidised pyrites) were also found in the north and south chambers of Chávez's tunnel. Ranging in width from 40 to 130mm, no one knows the purpose of these strange spheres. Like so much else about Teotihuacan, they leave us wondering.

The Nasca Lines

Huge imaginary and humanoid beings, gigantic geometric shapes, straight lines stretching for many kilometres, weird-looking plants, animals and insects etched into the high desert landscape of southern Peru ... the Nasca Lines are some of the most powerful, spectacular and mysterious human artworks ever created. One of the strangest things about these enigmatic designs is that in order to see them clearly and in full, the viewer needs to be high in the air, looking down on them. It is not possible to appreciate their beauty – or even to make much basic sense of the outlines – from the ground. How then, were they created? Why? And for whom?

The Lines, which occupy an area roughly 450 square kilometres in the arid Peruvian coastal plain south of Lima, are among world archaeology's greatest mysteries. Why can they only be properly visualised from altitude, and why are so many of them so extremely large? Many have tried to explain the origins and purpose of these geoglyphs. No one as yet has entirely succeeded.

Some have speculated that the extraordinary figures must be the work of shamans, who somehow directed their creation in the course of drug-inspired, out-of-body hallucinations. A more prosaic explanation might be that the ancient Nasca people, who flourished between c. AD 200 to 700, first sketched the works out on some kind of support, like vellum, and then, much in the way that modern crop circles can be created, scaled them up on the ground with the aid of ropes, mallets and wooden posts.

Another possibility is that the Nasca Lines had some kind of astronomical function, either in computing a calendar of cosmic events, or as part of some now long-forgotten ritual. Numerous broad track ways feature in the overall mix. They may have been made as processional avenues for large numbers of people.

Others have taken a much more imaginative, not to say challenging view, proposing that some of the long straight lines and other geometric shapes are 'runways' or landing grounds the Nasca people created either for gods, or for extraterrestrial visitors. Foremost among the proponents of this view was German writer Erich von Däniken. In his 1968 book *Chariots of the Gods*, von Däniken proposed that many ancient structures and artefacts were so far ahead of their time, they could only have been created by, or with help from, otherworldly beings.

Stonehenge, the Great Pyramid of Giza, the Easter Island *moai* and the Nasca Lines were among the many archaeological treasures von Däniken assumed must have enjoyed this extraterrestrial input. He believed the Nasca Lines were crude representations of alien structures that had once stood on Earth, and that they may have been created as a means of encouraging the extraterrestrials to return.

Then there is the idea that the Nasca geoglyphs mirror hidden underground watercourses, or act as some kind of ritual portals or pathways that help identify scarce water sources. Rainfall in the area is among the world's lowest: in some years, there is no rain at all. Given the perennial drought or near-drought conditions, it's easy to see where the idea came from that the search for water gave rise to the lines, or that they are connected to some kind of religious or ritual practice invoking rain.

The fan-shaped Nasca plain is bounded to the east by the foothills of the Andes Mountains, and enclosed elsewhere by three of the region's largest rivers. Whatever their reasons for undertaking these works, the artists who designed them used this flat, arid and extraordinary landscape as a massive creative arena. Once the shape had been decided, the builders simply scraped the topmost and darker layer of earth – known as 'desert varnish' – from the lighter underlying soil. Having exposed this and created the lines they wanted, they then placed the stones they had removed along either edge of the design to reinforce it.

Several of the straight lines run for many kilometres, while some of the trapezoid-shaped 'runways' are more than a kilometre in length. It is the extraordinary range and beauty of the biological forms, though, that really sticks in the memory. Among so many that are striking, a few stand out. One is a stick-thin, half-bent monkey. It seems to be gathering something in its paws from the ground. Created in one unbroken line and measuring more than 100 metres (328 feet) from side to side, it stands almost as tall as it is wide and has a superb, playful tail in the form of a tightly coiled spiral. Other unexplained geometric designs connect to the monkey figure, as if in obedience to some unknown and mysterious logic.

One of the more persuasive explanations for a number of the straight lines and tracks is that they act as midsummer or midwinter solstice markers – and in this way, as a kind of giant astronomical observatory. The lines and geometric shapes often either attach to or intercut the animal and other figures, almost as if these are terrestrial representations of some observed heavenly bodies. The Nasca people gave different names and configurations to the constellations we know as 'Ursa Major, the Great Bear', 'Taurus, the Bull', 'Canis Major', and so on.

Viewed in this light, the modern Western constellation we

known as 'Apus', meaning an 'exotic or extraordinary bird', may be one and the same as the massive bird-like creature that features in many descriptions of the lines. A cross between a supersized humming-bird and a giant pterodactyl, it measures more than 135 metres (443 feet) from the tip of its long pointed beak to the end of its slatted, triangular tail. There is also a magnificent spider, and the instantly recognisable outline of a killer whale. All of the geoglyphs are meticulously executed, and have survived for more than 2,000 years. One reason must be that there has been so little rain.

There are other monuments in the region that chime historically and artistically with the Nasca Lines. While they seem to share a similar aesthetic sensibility, these outlines were created on the slopes of foothills and mounds so that they could be viewed from below. The vast majority depict humanoid figures. Archaeologists believe they may be the work of the earlier Paracas and Topará cultures, which flourished between 500 BC and AD 200. They were created not by scraping off a layer of surface soil, but by placing stones in careful arrangements on the surface, and by piercing holes in the solid rock. Most striking are the strange and haunting 'faces' that are pecked into the slopes, like a child's drawing of a frightened adult.

The advent of drone technology is transforming archaeology, not least in Peru. In 2018, Peruvian archaeologists using drones discovered more than 50 new Nasca Lines in neighbouring Palpa province. So ancient and weathered they were too faint to be detected by the human eye, the new lines only became apparent by virtue of the drones' onboard 3-D, high-resolution mapping technology. The fresh discoveries may shed new light on the overall purpose and meaning of the lines as a whole.

Etching thousands of highly symbolic, magical-religious images and figures must have been the work of a strongly unified society that shared a powerful common stock of cultural, religious and ritual beliefs. Even allowing for the lack of rainfall, it is something of a miracle that the Lines have survived in such good condition up until the present day.

However they were planned and created, and whatever their original purpose might have been, the Nasca Lines are outstanding works of the collective human imagination, and fully deserve the UNESCO World Heritage status they enjoy. The best way to appreciate their full power and splendour is by overflying them in an aircraft, or from the basket of a hot air balloon. You could also take a trip to see them virtually on Google Earth. However you get up there, it will be worth it.

Easter Island

Let's think about it this way: suppose we were creating a new reality TV show. Two hundred handpicked volunteers have to survive on a small Pacific island in one of the world's most remote locations. They can come from anywhere in the world, they can split into teams of two or more, and if they want to the teams can even compete with each other. But everyone has to abide by the rules of the game.

The first rule is that they have to live in what amount to sixteenth-century conditions. This means no running water, no electricity, no modern health care, no modern communication devices of any kind, especially mobile telephones, and definitely no supermarkets. The teams will have to produce a reliable supply of food, and, since the work is extremely demanding, they will need to grow – and cook – a great deal of it.

Now that we've established the ground rules, let's move on to the challenge. Your mission is to carve a 10 metre (33ft) high, 82 tonne (90 ton) *moai* statue from the hard, glassy rock of a volcano. The location is Easter Island, and our teams are trying to replicate a task that its inhabitants, the Rapa Nui (the original name both for the islanders and for Easter Island itself) managed to achieve not just once, but hundreds of times in the course of many centuries.

The statue must be the highly stylised but recognisable representation of an important ancestor (they will have to agree between themselves which of their respective ancestors to choose). The sculpture must also have award-winning artistic merit, feature a disproportionately large head exactly three-eighths the size of the whole figure, and have extremely long ears.

What are the chances of our volunteers coping? Maybe not all that great. In the first place, they will have to agree on some kind of leadership, or failing that, on a completely flat organisa-tion that will not break down into squabbles, sulks and outright conflict brought about by rivalry, one-upmanship, laziness, sexual jealousy, hunger, violence, disease or any of the myriad other problems that can plague this type of human venture.

Once they've chipped this enormous icon from the bedrock using nothing more than stone tools, and carved it to the judges' liking, our contestants have to polish it with pumice stone until its surface is glistening and beautifully smooth. They must then decorate it with incised lines and highlight parts of it in brightly coloured paints they have manufactured themselves.

The next task is to transport the monolith several miles across rough ground to the coast without damaging it, and set it upright on an *ahu*. This is a massive, dry-stone platform that must be built in good time for the installation of the finished statue, and be completed as a separate undertaking.

To make things even more interesting, all the work must be done without metal implements of any kind; with only the cord-age the volunteers can fashion out of natural fibres; and they must scour the island to find enough large trees to provide the timber that might help in moving the *moai* they have created to its final resting place.

Obviously, they will have to agree on the division of labour – some to plant and harvest food, some to cook, others to chip the rock, an artistic team to oversee and ensure creative brilliance, or some kind of rota for managing these separate tasks in a fair way, taking into account the various talents and demands of the people involved.

The teams will also have to find some way of dealing with incidents and accidents, such as broken legs and crushed fingers, without bringing the whole enterprise to a juddering halt. But as we elaborate the scenario, it's clear that even if they do somehow manage to hew, lever and cajole a 90-ton idol from the volcano's flanks without murdering one another, of all the difficulties that confront them, the greatest will be working out a way of moving the completed statue across the island to the *ahu* rock platform. If they do succeed in getting it there in one piece, they then have to set it upright, and, as a final challenge, perch on its head a jaunty, cylindrical red hat, several tons in weight, cut separately from scoria, a different type of rock. (The system known as 'parbuckling' might just come in useful here.)

Even thinking about making and moving a *moai* under these conditions makes us nervous – what would Health & Safety have to say? The obvious difficulty of the enterprise has led some commentators to doubt that the Rapa Nui people themselves could possibly have done it, on the grounds that they 'must have lacked the necessary sophistication', or however else that dismissal is phrased.

More extreme claims include the highly fanciful notion that extraterrestrials must have created the *moai* in situ, or somehow 'brought' them to the island. In reality, expressing doubts of the kind is both patronising and essentially racist. It's clear that in employing specialist skills they had evolved and built up over many generations, the people of Easter Island became experts in their chosen art. But we're still left with the conundrum of *how* even these experts moved the giant *moai* across the island. Various theories have been put forward: the figures were laid face up on log rollers and pushed, and/or dragged; they were lashed to wooden sledges, which were placed on log rollers, and they were pulled and pushed along with the rearmost logs being carried to the front of the sledge once they had emerged at the back. Animal fat helped make things easier. This is a favourite explanation both for how the Stonehenge monoliths were transported, and the great blocks of stone that make up the Great Pyramid. It's certainly how nineteenth-century archaeological entrepreneur and showman 'The Great Belzoni' stole the Egyptian Colossus we can currently see in the British Museum.

Others are convinced that each statue has its own biography: each represents the most revered and important ancestors of a tribe or family group, and each was moved to its final resting place in the manner that was best suited to the individual statue, taking into account factors like its weight, its centre of gravity, the clan that was moving it and the exact nature of the intervening terrain.

If the experts are right, and the *moai* are 'chiefly the living faces (*aringa ora*) of deified ancestors (*aringa ora ata tepuna*)', then the dead tribal chiefs or elders are sentinels. Their spirits forever encapsulated in these wonderful stone images, the dead watch over the living and ensure their survival.

This interpretation is borne out by two things: first, the fact that following the series of disasters that befell the Rapa Nui as a result of contact with the outside world, they lowered the statues to the ground and placed them face downwards – as if to spare their ancestors the pain of witnessing the misery that had overtaken them. Second, and contrary to what the television programmes tend to make us believe, many of the *moai* do not gaze out to sea as if awaiting some kind of deliverance from afar; the vast majority look inwards onto the communities that built them.

The Rapa Nui also built a series of astronomical observatories known as *tupa* at key vantage points along a north–south axis across the island. Entered by crawling through a very narrow passageway, the *tupa* may have helped calculate the most propitious dates in the calendar for contacting the spirits of the ancestors. If this is true, then at these special times the statues were endowed with life by means of ritual ceremonies.

The true unsolved mystery of Easter Island, then, may not be what the *moai* represent, but how they were moved. How did the Rapa Nui, who, between AD 1200 and 1600 built almost 900 *moai* figures, actually transport these stone colossi from the source quarry on the slopes of Rano Rararku, a slumbering volcano about two miles from the south-eastern coast of the island, to their final locations? Especially the gigantic, super-heavy ones that were carefully aligned in rows of up to 15 on the coastal *ahu*, the massive dry-stone platforms that provide a kind of theatrical stage for more than 400 of the figures?

In 1955, Norwegian explorer Thor Heyerdahl landed on Rapa Nui to investigate the 'Easter Island Faces' as many people then called them. Initially, Heyerdahl failed to realise that, to ensure stability, the lower two-thirds of the inland statues are actually buried, making the task of moving them very much more difficult than he had anticipated. Undeterred, Heyerdahl organised a large-scale experiment: about 180 of the islanders laid a statue on its back, roped it up and dragged it a few hundred yards along one of the '*moai* roads' that starburst out across the island from the quarry. It immediately became clear that this way of doing things would badly damage the figures. However hard they tried, the Norwegian explorer and his team were not able to solve the puzzle of how the Rapa Nui managed to move the *moai* without inflicting so much as a scratch. It was as if they had summoned some unworldly magic, and caused them to float across the ground. The most interesting, as well as one of the most recent suggestions, is that the *moai* 'walked'.

A few years ago, two American archaeologists noticed a

difference between what they called the 'road *moai*' – the mostly smaller statues either lying or positioned near to one or other of the island's long-established tracks – and the mostly larger statues that were set up on the coastal *ahu* plinths. The researchers reasoned that the road *moai* were never meant to be moved. But the statues that had been set up on the *ahu* platforms looked different to their roadside cousins, and looked as if they might have been. Generally larger in size, they all had a slightly rounded base and a lower centre of gravity; and they all looked as if they were leaning slightly forwards.

In a moment of remarkable insight, the archaeologists wondered: what if you could make a statue move by tying ropes around its head? Two or more teams of people would use these to begin rocking the statue gently from side to side. Gradually, working in close harmony, the teams could build up the range and speed of the rocking motion until the *moai* took life, and began to walk on its rounded base. To test their theory, the researchers created a scaled-down, but still very heavy version of a *moai*, and attached long ropes to either side of it. A dozen or so people handled each of these. A third team of volunteers positioned behind the statue controlled a third rope to prevent the figure from toppling forward. To the delight and amazement of everyone concerned, theory became reality. Wobbling along like some gigantic children's toy, the statue sauntered happily along a stretch of unpaved track, for all the world as if it were going for a post-dinner constitutional. It even managed to 'walk' up a slight incline, suffering no damage to its upper surfaces in the process. Viewing the video footage of a *moai* moving in this oddly human way is electrifying – you can't help feeling that the statue is in some way truly alive.

The experiment could explain how the smaller of the *moai* were moved. But does it really tell us how the truly colossal statues destined for pride of place on the *ahu*, were transported? It seems unlikely. And it certainly doesn't explain how they were raised onto the platforms from which they maintain their eternal watch. There is still so much left to learn in the world. And so little time left to do it.

The Loch Ness Monster

Many of us would be disappointed if it turned out that the modern incarnation of the Loch Ness Monster had been born in a London pub. Yet that is exactly what a writer named Digby George Gerahty tells us happened. In his 1950 novel *Marise*, written under the pen name Stephen Lister, Gerahty's own, thinly veiled persona meets a French gendarme who has come to find out if he is hiding a lion on his property. Gerahty tells him, *mais non, Monsieur*, there are no large wild beasts wandering about in my shrubbery. But, 'you may accept my assurance that the Loch Ness Monster was born in my presence, during a conversation which took place in a London public house . . . The Loch Ness Monster was invented for a fee of £150 by an ingenious publicity man.'

Professor Henry Bauer, a cryptozoologist and true believer in Nessie's existence, unearthed this blatant and extraordinary confession. Bauer, who despite his faith in the beast liked to smoke out a monster fraud if it was smouldering, came upon *Marise* after diligent searching. Intrigued by the comments in the novel that bear on the Loch Ness Monster's apparent invention, Bauer contacted Gerahty and asked him to explain them. In the subsequent conversation, Gerahty admitted that he himself was the 'ingenious publicity man' in question. He said that in the spring of 1933, 'a group of hotel owners in the area of Lossiemouth' had hired him to find a way of improving the tourist trade, which had all but died away as a consequence of the Great Depression.

At the time the hoteliers supposedly approached him, and by complete coincidence, Gerahty said he had another client who ran an estate agency in British Columbia's Okanagan Valley. This man claimed to have invented a lake monster he christened Ogopogo (no, really), to boost the local tourist footprint. The agent said that, in spite of the lake creature's obviously fictitious name, the scheme had worked far better than he could ever have imagined, with people coming from far and wide in the hope of catching a glimpse of the mysterious Ogopogo, which didn't and never had existed – except in the fertile loam of the estate agent's imagination.

Inspired by this example, and, 'over several pints of beer', Gerahty told Bauer: 'We became midwives of the reborn Loch Ness Monster. All we had to do was arrange for the monster to be sighted. This we did and the story snowballed. Thousands went north to see it, and [see it] they did. It was, of course, pure hokum.'

Is Gerahty's confession true? He died shortly after talking to Bauer, and without revealing any further information – for example, the name or names of the stooges who subsequently agreed to 'sight' a monster in Loch Ness. Whether or not Gerahty was behind it, sure enough, on 2 May 1933, the *Inverness Courier* ran an article headed: 'Strange spectacle in Loch Ness. What was it?' The report, by 'A Correspondent', who preferred to remain anonymous, claimed that a couple driving along the western shore of the loch near Abriachan Pier had seen something creating a 'tremendous upheaval' in the middle of the loch. While they also remained coyly unnamed, the article said the travellers were 'a well-known local businessman' and his 'University graduate wife'. Good credentials, then – a university education obviously precludes any chance of deceit. The couple stopped the car and got out to watch as 'the creature disported itself, rolling and plunging for fully a minute, its body resembling that of a whale, and the water cascading and churning like a simmering cauldron.'

The modern legend of the Loch Ness Monster picked up more popular traction on the afternoon of 22 July 1933, when another couple driving around the loch, this time Londoners Mr and Mrs George Spicer, reported seeing a large, unknown creature resembling 'a huge snail with a long neck' crossing the road in front of them from left to right. It then disappeared down the slope towards the loch. At the time, the Spicers were motoring down the east side of Loch Ness, about halfway between Dores and Foyers on General Wade's Military Road.

George Spicer sent a letter describing what they had seen to the very same *Inverness Courier* that had reported the Abriachan Pier encounter. In the letter, which was published on 4 August, Mr Spicer said: '[I]t was the nearest approach to a dragon or prehistoric monster that I have seen in my life . . . It appeared to be carrying a small lamb or animal of some kind. It seemed to have a long neck, which moved up and down in the manner of a scenic railway, and the body was fairly big with a high back . . . Length from six to eight feet and very ugly.'

Interviewed later, Spicer claimed that in his concern not to exaggerate, he had deliberately played down the creature's size. In fact, when the 12 feet width of the road at that point was made clear to him, he agreed that the 'dragon' must have been more like 25 feet in length.

In November of that same very busy year for Nessie, a man named Hugh Gray presented what he said was the very first photograph of the Loch Ness Monster. In a statement to the press, Gray described it as a '40-foot serpent'. While many accepted the snap at face value, others felt the fuzzy, poorly focused image looked like nothing so much as a Labrador dog swimming towards the camera with a curved stick in its mouth. From this time on, arguments over the authenticity of Nessie sightings and photographs would only increase in frequency and heat.

On 5 January 1934, motorcyclist Arthur Grant reported a second sighting of a strange, antediluvian beast lurking by the roadside, once again on the outskirts of Abriachan. This triggered the tourist invasion that the originators of the hoax – if indeed it is a hoax – had been hoping for. Visitors began flocking to the loch, eager to try and catch a glimpse of the monster for themselves.

A pattern was beginning to emerge, that would continue right through the remainder of 1933 and well on into 1935: local people and tourists reported sightings of Nessie; the *Inverness Courier* and other local outlets published the details; the stories were picked up by the national and international press; the story of the monster in the loch snowballed; and the hotels began to fill. Not, sadly, in Lossiemouth, to the chagrin of the hoteliers who had supposedly commissioned the deception in the first place, but at the northern end of the loch in and around Inverness.

As monster fever grew and the opportunity for a large increase in sales beckoned, in December 1933 the *Daily Mail* newspaper hired one-time big game hunter, film-maker and silent movie star Marmaduke ('Duke') Wetherell to lead an investigation seeking hard evidence of Nessie's existence. Within a matter of days, Wetherell had apparently fulfilled his commission by 'discovering' the tracks of a large, unidentified animal on the edge of the loch south of Foyers. Disappointment followed the initial excitement at the extraordinary find: Natural History Museum experts in London swiftly identified the plaster casts of the footprints as having all been made by the same, left, hind foot of a hippopotamus. What was a hippopotamus doing in

Scotland? And why did it only have one foot? It turned out that Wetherell had faked the 'monster' tracks with a hippopotamus foot umbrella stand. Having caught Wetherell out in this blatant attempt to fool everyone, the *Daily Mail* dismissed him from the investigation. His son, Ian, said that his father came back home seething. Wetherell's anger only increased when the *Mail* then ridiculed him publicly for trying to pull the stunt. Ranting, 'We'll give them their monster', 'the Duke' set about hatching a plan for revenge. (It is hard to believe that he omitted an expletive before uttering the word 'monster'.)

By coincidence, Marmaduke Wetherell's stepbrother, Christian Spurling, was an accomplished artist and model-maker. In a bizarre act of pique it would be impossible to invent, 'the Duke' asked Spurling to create a fake, but convincing Loch Ness Monster.

The result of this hoax, the 'Surgeon's Photograph' became one of the most famous images of all time. Published in the *Daily Mail* on 21 April 1934, it has been viewed by millions of people worldwide. For more than 60 years, many believed it was a real shot of Nessie, sticking her long, arched neck up out of the water as if to say, 'All right, Mr DeMille, I'm ready for my close up.'

On 7 December 1975, the *Sunday Telegraph* newspaper published its 'Sunday Morning with Mandrake' column. In the piece, 'Mandrake' – the pen name of journalist Peter Purser – revealed how Marmaduke Wetherell, his son Ian and his stepbrother had perpetrated the hoax. Spurling fashioned a Plesiosaurus-like head, neck and upper back out of plastic wood, and then glued this to the conning tower of a tinplate, clockwork toy submarine they'd bought for two-shillings-and-sixpence from Woolworth's department store in Richmond, West London. Once the fake had been painted grey and was ready for launch, Ian Wetherell drove his father and a photographer friend, Maurice Chambers, up to Loch Ness on or about 19 April 1934. According to Ian they 'found an inlet where the tiny ripples would look like full size waves out on the loch, and with the actual scenery in the background. Then it was just a matter of winding up the sub and getting it to dive just below the surface so the neck and head drew a proper little "V" in the water.'

Ian Wetherell took five photographs of the fake monster with his Leica camera, only just managing to grab them before a water bailiff came along to ask them what they were doing. To prevent the bailiff from spotting their clockwork Nessie, Marmaduke stood on the model and sank it. It was a near miss, but they got away with it. Chambers sent the snaps Ian had taken off to be developed. He then rephotographed two of them using his own, professional quarter-plate camera. One of the resulting prints was sensational. A clear winner in every sense of the term, it became 'The Surgeon's Photograph'.

At this point, the London surgeon in question, 35-year-old Dr Robert K. Wilson, MB, B.Chir. (Cantab), FRCS (Edinburgh) enters the story. Friendly with photographer and upmarket salesman Chambers (who couldn't in any way be described as flashy, but drove a bright yellow Rolls-Royce), Wilson agreed to act as the credible source of the 'monster' photograph.

Chambers loaned Wilson his bulky camera, which came complete with leather bellows, a magazine containing four 8 x 10cm glass plates coated with photographic emulsion, and was anything but easy to operate. Wilson, on his own account, was no photographer. But that did not matter, as the surgeon didn't have to bother taking any photographs at all in the course of his drive up to northern Scotland. In fact, he didn't even stop at Loch Ness. Instead, as agreed with his fellow conspirators, he drove directly to Ogston's chemist shop in Union Street, Inverness. He handed the exposed 'fake monster' plates Chambers had given him in London to the shopkeeper, George Morrison, and went for a coffee while he awaited the results.

Viewing the developed prints, Morrison's eyebrows came in for a bit of extra lifting. He immediately realised that one of them was of world-changing significance. He advised the customer who had brought them in to forget about the local *Inverness Courier* newspaper, and sell the extraordinary image lying on the counter between them to the highest bidder in Fleet Street. Wilson agreed, and, again as had been planned, drove the newly developed photographs all the way back down to London again. Not surprisingly, the *Daily Mail*, which had commissioned the Great Monster Expedition in the first place, offered him £100 for the snaps, or some £6,000 in today's money. Unfortunately for Wilson, the British Medical Association fined him £1,000 – £60,000 in today's money – for allowing his name to be used in substantiating them.

A better person for this validation could hardly have been found: Wilson's background and credentials were impeccable. He appeared to be the epitome of Establishment values. A reservist Lt. Colonel in the Royal Army Medical Corps, as a young First World War volunteer he had been wounded in action in France, and mentioned in Dispatches for conspicuous bravery. Why did this well-respected gynaecologist, with a lucrative private practice in Queen Anne Street, central London, agree to act as an agent of mass deception?

Once the story broke, and the astonishing photograph had appeared on the front page of just about every newspaper in the world, everyone wanted Wilson to give chapter and verse on how he had captured one of the most iconic images of all time. Wilson, however, proved to be a very reluctant witness. He told the press he didn't want publicity. He was just a medical man, and an amateur photographer who had simply happened to get lucky in the course of a tourist jaunt. Far from discouraging attention, Wilson's modesty and his persistent desire to stay out of the limelight served further to convince many observers that he was a credible, not to say unimpeachable, witness. The vast majority of people believed that Wilson had actually seen the Loch Ness Monster, snapped it, and that the photograph was real. Former Nessie sceptics were converted to the cause, as were millions of people worldwide. The Loch Ness Monster existed, and here was the absolute, unshakable proof.

Much later, the bashful surgeon gave an account of his supposed sighting of the monster to writer Constance Whyte. Herself a qualified doctor, long-term Nessie biographer Whyte was a founding member of the Loch Ness Phenomenon Investigation Bureau (LNPIB) and author of *More Than a Legend*. Published in 1957, the book was a compendium of what was known about the monster up until that time. In the course of an interview intended to update it, Wilson told Whyte:

I had a fast car in those days, and after travelling all night arrived at Fort Augustus too early to get breakfast, so decided to go on to Inverness . . .

At about 7 or 7:30 a.m., I stopped by the roadside two or three miles on the Inverness side of Invermoriston, at a point where the road is some one hundred feet above the loch. I had got over the dyke and was standing a few yards down the slope and looking towards the loch when I noticed a considerable commotion on the surface, perhaps two or three hundred yards out. When I had watched it for perhaps a minute or so, something broke surface and I saw the head of some strange animal rising out of the water.

I hurried to the car for my camera, then went down and along the steep bank for about fifty yards to get a better view and focused on something which was moving through the water. I was too busy managing the camera to make accurate observation, but I made four exposures, by which time the object had completely disappeared. I had no idea at the time whether I had anything on the plates or not, but thought I might have.

Wilson's entire account of this journey and his encounter with the Loch Ness Monster was a fabrication. The curious thing about the exposure of the hoax is that, for many of the fans who believed in Nessie's existence, it served only to reinforce, and not, if you can forgive the unintended pun, to scotch the legend. As for the 'Surgeon's Photograph', it resulted in a very big increase in visitor numbers to Loch Ness.

The success of Wetherell's prank encouraged many others to try their luck in similar ways, including the author of the 1951 'triple hump' photograph. This turned out to consist of three tarpaulin-covered straw bales, floated in the shallows at the edge of the loch and snapped in a way that made it look as if they were far offshore. Over the years, more and more people have sought to exploit the legend by creating imaginary and sometimes very inventive representations of the monster. A Loch Ness boat tour operator, who used fibreglass for the purpose, created the most recent fake Nessie in 2015.

Leaving aside Gerahty's claims to have reinvented the monster for the modern age, Nessie-spotting has been going on for a long time. Many, including the eminent naturalist Sir Peter Scott, have discovered it can become compulsive. In some cases, this has been at the cost of their better reputations.

The first known written record of a monster at Loch Ness dates back to Adomnán's *Life of St Columba*. Written around AD 700, Chapter 28 of this early written work tells us that when St Columba was preaching 'in the province of the Picts', he needed to cross the river Nesam, or Ness: '*Alio cumque in tempore, cum vir beatus in Pictorum provincia per aliquot moraretur dies, necesse habuit fluvium transire Nesam,*' is what the Latin actually says. 'And then another time, when the saint had decided to spend a few days in the province of the Picts, he needed to cross the river Ness.' But when he reached the riverbank, the saint saw a group of locals burying a man who had just been savagely bitten to death by a monster that had reared up from the deep. Undeterred, and certain that God would help him in case of need, St Columba told one of his followers, Lugneus Mocumin, to swim across and bring back the skiff or coble (*caupallum*) he could see moored to the bank on the far side.

As Lugneus made his way across the river, the monster sensed the disturbance. Surging up with a mighty roar, it was just about to eat the hapless monk when St Columba made the sign of the cross in the air and ordered the ferocious beast to desist. Struck by the power of the Lord, the terrifying apparition slunk back down to its horrid, watery lair. To paraphrase Adomnán, 'all who were terrified, including the barbarians present, gave thanks for the miracle and praised the greatness of the Christian faith.' The 'barbarians', in this case, meant the astonished Picts. It would be uncharitable to cast any doubt or aspersions on the rectitude of a saint, but this wasn't the first time St Columba had used his miraculous powers to prevent heathens coming to any harm in an emergency, thereby winning over new converts to the Christian faith – and nor would it be the last.

The next eyewitness account of a strange creature in Loch Ness was written down by Walter of Bingham, a twelfth-century monk who has been very aptly described as 'Scotland's answer to Marco Polo'. Inspired by his mentor, Gerald of Wales, Walter decided to make a pilgrimage to the holy sites of Scotland. Even better for posterity, he made a careful record, complete with drawings, of his journey through ancient Caledonia. The result is a unique, twelfth-century Scottish travelogue.

Luckily for us, one of Walter's most striking entries records another early encounter with the Loch Ness Monster. The action once again takes place on the banks of a river that runs into the eponymous loch. As before, Walter wants to cross, and first asks a group of nearby fishermen mending their nets if they will take him. They refuse in a way that suggests they are terrified, but won't tell him of what.

Walter walks on down the river, where he meets a boy pulling a small boat or coracle on a length of rope. The youth demands a silver coin as payment for ferrying our monk to the other side, which Walter, who admits to being parsimonious, is at first reluctant to pay. The deal once concluded, Walter and the boy make it safely across the river.

Then, as the boy sets out on the return journey and Walter looks on in horror, 'a huge beast with flames shooting from its eyes' rears up out of the water, gives vent to an ear-splitting roar, and drags both the boy and his boat beneath the waves.

The drawing in Walter's manuscript was faded almost to the point of invisibility, but scientists using a pioneering technique known as Re-Zoom Spectroscopy (RZS) took multiple photographs of the image, overlaid them one on top of another and then processed the result using a 'Guggenheim manipulator'. The British Library claims the rather wonderful result as the earliest known, if somewhat enhanced, image of Nessie. As an educated cleric, though, Walter might just have been retelling, if not directly plagiarising, Adomnán's earlier, very similar, account.

Dozens of supposed photographs of Nessie and hundreds of feet of film and video have been shot over the years. None of them has been accepted as incontrovertible scientific evidence of the monster's existence. Even so, among the more than 2,000 purported Nessie clips posted on YouTube, there have been some entertaining if not wholly convincing videos of great,

The Shepherd's Monument. Will anyone be able to crack the Shugborough Code?

Right: Göbekli Tepe. Where it all began – the most mysterious place on Earth.

Below: Göbekli Tepe. Does this vulture hold a comet in its hands? Or a human skull?

Stonehenge Stones. Looks like a film set: the bluestone outcrop at Craig Rhos-y-felin.

Above: Teotihuacan. Steeped in blood: the sacrificial pyramids of Teotihuacan.

Right: Teotihuacan. Imbued with a strange, brooding power – jade figurines discovered at Teotihuacan.

Easter Island. Lost horizons – what do the *moai* see?

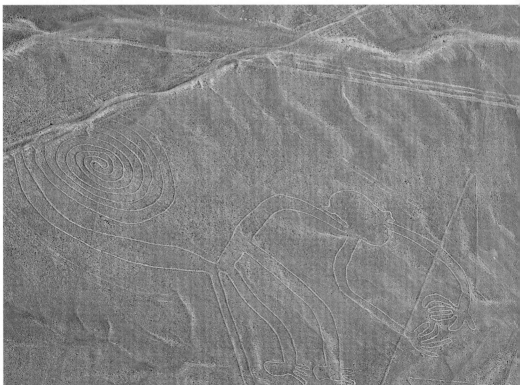

The Nasca Lines. Enchanting creatures – but you can only see them from on high.

The Loch Ness Monster. A model monster:
'. . . ready for my close-up.'

The Phaistos Disc. Do we really know
what the disc is telling us?

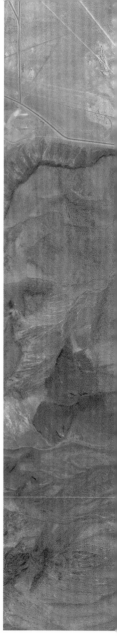

Above: Is there life on Mars? An aerial view of Area 51.

Left: The remains of a flying saucer – or a Cold War spy balloon?

The Rising Star
Cave. *Homo naledi*
– Gollum walked the
Earth; our strangest
ancestor.

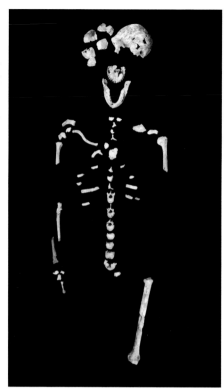

The Zodiac killer.
Taunting the police,
and getting away
with it: a Zodiac
cryptogram.

Sorry I haven't written,

but I just washed my pen...

beast-like entities that seem to be swimming on or just below the surface of the loch.

Numerous sonar surveys of the waters, which are notoriously murky on account of the loch's high peat content, have also been carried out, notably Operation Deepscan, which was organised by ecologist and long-standing Nessie-watcher Adrian Shine in October 1987. It involved a line of some 20 sonar-equipped boats steaming up the loch in unison, scanning the depths for signs of life. They did not find any. Samples retrieved during a further, very thorough, slow sonar survey of the loch's heavily silted bottom in 2008 once again provided no evidence of a large aquatic animal living there, either alive or dead.

The steep hills that surround much of the loch can create sudden rushes and downdraughts of air that can claw at the loch's surface, creating 'cat's paws' that appear to be solid objects travelling at speed. This is especially true when a strong wind is blowing sideways across the loch. Boat wakes can also create 'lumps' or folds on the loch's surface, especially on calm days. These can remain visible even when the boat in question has disappeared from view. As to all the 'monstrous commotions' that have been reported over the years, local loch boat skippers like Captain John McDonald, who travelled up and down the loch some 20,000 times in the space of a 50-year career, are dismissive. McDonald says these are nothing more than shoals of large salmon, which often swim in long columns, leaping in and out of the water as they go.

If a large aquatic animal really does live in the loch, then what is it? A carnivorous marine reptile scientists believe went extinct about 65 million years ago, fossil-based reconstructions of the *Plesiosaurus* fit best with most of the eyewitness descriptions. Wikipedia tells us that '*Plesiosaurus* is a genus of extinct, large marine *sauropterygian* reptile that lived during the early part of the Jurassic Period ... It is distinguishable by its small head, long and slender neck, broad, turtle-like body, a short tail and two pairs of large, elongated paddles.' This description tallies well with the majority of Nessie sightings. (Some scientists believe *Plesiosaurus* was swimming about in the oceans much earlier, around 200 million years ago during the Late Triassic era – but what's a few million years between experts?)

There are, though, a few problems with the *Plesiosaurus* theory. One is that the current surface of Loch Ness, a landlocked feature carved out by glacial action many thousands of years ago, sits some 16 metres (52.4ft) *above* sea level. Some experts nonetheless claim that as the ice melted around 14,000 years ago, there was a relatively brief window of time during which the North Sea and the waters of the loch were connected. Did this allow a posse of plesiosaurs to swim up the Great Glen, and set up a permanent home in the loch? Did they then become trapped there as the ice retreated? A marine clamshell dredged up recently by a clay-fouled anchor near Castle Urquhart was scientifically dated to 14,100 BC. This fits exactly with the time of the last glacial melt, and the accompanying rise in global sea levels. The shell, then, lends some credence to the idea that there was a period during which the sea and what is now Loch Ness were joined together. Yet the plesiosaurs could not have survived over the millennia as a single family. In order to thrive, substantial numbers of the creatures would have had to make the initial journey, and then breed successfully with one another for thousands of years.

The fact that the current loch is a freshwater and not a saltwater lake also argues against the idea that Nessie is a *Plesiosaurus*, a species that lived in the sea. In answer to this objection, Nessie enthusiasts retort that the creatures simply adapted to the water's changing salinity over the years. On a further intriguing note, more and more dinosaur footprints are being discovered at various locations in Scotland, not least on the Isle of Skye, where the 170 million-year-old footprints of Middle Jurassic sauropods such as *Brontosaurus* and theropods like *Tyrannosaurus rex* continue to emerge from the fossilised mud.

The waters of Urquhart Bay, which in some places run more than 700 feet deep, are where the majority of Nessie sightings have been made. Two small rivers enter the loch here, providing a renewable food source in the shape of salmon and trout. Again, though, some experts argue there are simply not enough fish in the loch to keep a viable number of plesiosaurs alive for more than a short time.

The very many first-hand sightings of the Loch Ness Monster work against this scepticism. In his excellent book on the subject, author Gareth Williams tells us: '[B]y the mid-1970s, an estimated 10,000 people had reported seeing the monster. Skimming off the obviously mad and bad left a hard core of roughly 3,000 sightings that seem plausible.' That's one hell of a lot of sightings. And even if you set the 'plausible' reports against the experiment in which Adrian Shine randomly raised and lowered a wooden post out of the water, causing one-third of observers to report that they had seen something other than a piece of wood, that still leaves some 2,000 credible eyewitnesses. If questioned, they will tell you that they not only saw the monster, they will readily swear to it.

Also working for the monster's existence is the sheer size and depth of Loch Ness. Plummeting to deeps of 230 metres (755ft) and with a surface area of 56km² (22 sq. miles), it contains more fresh water than all of the lakes in England and Wales put together. It is the largest body of water in Scotland's Great Glen, which runs along a geological fault-line from Inverness in the north-east to Fort William in the south-west. A 1970 sonar mapping of the loch discovered that, in total contradiction to all previous bathythermic surveys, Loch Ness conceals, in Williams' words, 'an astonishing underwater landscape of ridges, canyons [over 400 feet deep in places] – and caverns – some of which [are] big enough to conceal an animal up to 30 feet in length.'

While the numbers of sightings have dramatically fallen off in the decades since the 1930s, with every new generation, the fascination with Loch Ness and its possible inhabitants takes new forms. In June 2018, in an effort to prove or disprove the existence of the monster, a team of scientists from the University of Otago, New Zealand, began looking for environmental DNA (eDNA) in the loch. The researchers will take samples of water from three different depths at different areas of Loch Ness. Environmental DNA is nuclear, or mitochondrial DNA that is found in a given environment. Among other things, it is secreted from the skin, carcasses, mucus, faeces and hair of organisms. Using the quantitative Polymerase Chain Reaction (qPCR) technique, eDNA can be detected at very low concentrations in water samples. While eDNA in open water may not persist for more than ten days, eDNA trapped in sediment can be preserved for thousands of years.

Everyone will get very excited if the investigation finds evidence of any ancient and long-thought-extinct species – like, for example a *Plesiosaurus*. Or perhaps even a mutant variation of said creature. To ensure scientific rigour, the team will take separate samples from various locations in nearby Loch Morar, Loch Garry and Loch Oich and have them separately tested as controls. To make absolutely sure there is no mistake nor any possibility of fiddling the results, all of the samples will go to laboratories in France, the US, Denmark, Australia and New Zealand. There, researchers ignorant of where each sample came from will test them blind. Once the eDNA from all the samples has been sequenced, it will be compared against international databases of known species. If there really is an unknown 'monster' species in Loch Ness, then its eDNA should show up. Even if the species is completely unknown to science, the evidence could still be used to determine to which class of animal it belongs. The results of the survey are not expected to be ready until some time in 2019.

Whether or not it exists, the Loch Ness Monster is big business, generating about £25 million a year for the local economy. Many people have a vested interest in keeping the legend alive, and if the one million annual visitors to the area and the 200,000 or so monthly Google searches for the monster are anything to go by, they have little to worry about. Surveys show that 85 per cent of visitors arrive in the hope of spotting Nessie.

Thousands of Nessie fans around the world regularly check in to one or other of the 24/7 webcams that watch the waters of the loch. Will one of these devotees or a scientific team ever find universally accepted proof of the Loch Ness Monster's existence? The revelation would be truly and sublimely wonderful.

Bigfoot and Other Suspects

As we've seen with the Loch Ness Monster, nothing divides people into believers and non-believers quite so much as a cryptid, which is to say, 'an animal whose existence or survival is disputed or unsubstantiated'. Of these, the giant hairy ape-like creature known as 'Bigfoot' or the 'Sasquatch' is one of the best-known and most controversial examples.

Bigfoot Believers contend that, in the time since its existence was first mooted, there have been thousands of sightings, signs, footprint casts, photographs and film footage of the world-famous creature. These are almost all said to have been recorded in wild reaches of forest, and in many regions of the United States and Canada. Given the vast number and variety of these reports, enthusiasts also contend that it is unscientific not to believe outright in the creature's existence. Or, at the very least, that the accumulated evidence warrants serious scientific investigation. Many others, among them a good dusting of bioscientists and anthropologists, dismiss the whole Bigfoot story out of hand. They view it as a hoax, or a folk tale, that began in modern times as a practical joke, and then took on a life of its own.

If the Bigfoot legend is a hoax, then how was it perpetrated? The best-known story goes that on Wednesday, 27 August 1958 a man named Jerry Crew was clearing brush and tree stumps at the leading edge of a new timber access road north of Willow Creek, in Del Norte County, Northern California.

Bordered by the Pacific Ocean to the west and Oregon to the north, Del Norte is renowned for its highly diverse and flourishing flora and fauna, among them the world-famous redwood trees (*Sequoia sempervirens*) that march in massive, towering regiments along its north-western coastal strip.

Moving inland from the mighty legions of redwood, the 1,230 square miles (3,200km²) region is also home to the wild and rugged Klamath mountain range. Its peaks reach as high as 9,029 feet (2,752m), it is very sparsely populated, and the soil and the prevailing climate provide ideal growing conditions for one of the widest ranges of conifer species in the world. These dense forests – many of them now designated national parks – are home to bobcats, mountain lions, lynx, black bears, pine martens and many other more or less fearsome creatures besides. With lots of trees, lots of animals and very few people, vast stretches of this region are classified as areas of outright wilderness.

What we don't know, we tend to fear – which is why so many tales of ghosts and gremlins, goblins and monsters, witches and warlocks have their roots firmly planted in wild, uninhabited stretches of land: especially dense tracts of dark and inaccessible forest. The Grimm brothers' tale of *Hansel and Gretel* is a good example.

Returning to our own account, we find 'catskinner' Jerry Crew, of good family, and from the nearby hamlet of Salyer, at the controls of a Caterpillar tractor. Complete with a bulldozer blade, it is helping clear and grade the land for the new, federally funded Bluff Creek Road. The local Wallace Brothers Logging Company is building this under subcontract. People who knew him described Crew as a sober and solid citizen, with glossy-black, short-cut hair and a broad chest. The one thing that made him stand out was his prominent ears. He was not known for playing practical jokes.

According to Marian T. Place, in her 1974 book *On the Track of Bigfoot*, Jerry honked his horn in greeting at his boss, Wilbur 'Shorty' Wallace, on arrival that morning, and then drove on to where he had left his bulldozer. As he changed into his work clothes and hard hat, Jerry noticed a set of large, odd-looking tracks printed deep into the soft earth next to the machine. He climbed up onto the tractor and looked down. From this higher point of vantage, the footprints no longer looked odd – they looked impossibly large. Much too large to have been made by human feet. They also appeared to have five separate, and strikingly human-like, toes. Mystified, Crew knew they could not be the tracks of a bear.

Wondering whether he might be the victim of a practical joke, Crew went back to tell Shorty Wallace what he'd seen. Some of the other men gathered round to listen – a fact that is in itself suspicious, and suggests a set-up of the type Jerry had immediately thought. Wallace told his apparently rapt audience – there were some 30 men on site that day – that whatever had left the giant tracks might be responsible for some of the mysterious goings-on at the lumber camp over the past few weeks. On one occasion, a huge, 700lb spare tyre for the road-grading machine had somehow ended up in a ditch; another time, someone – or something – had apparently tossed a full, 450lb drum of diesel fuel over the side of a bluff into a gully.

As they chewed over what, if anything, the unfeasibly large footprints could be, the men coined the name 'Big Foot' (at this stage, composed of two separate words) to label the possible culprit. Marian Place goes on to say that Shorty Wallace 'winked broadly' to break up the discussion, and told the men 'to be sure and let him know if they saw any apes skedaddling through the timber'. Meantime, he'd 'sure appreciate it if you got to work'. His mention of 'apes' at this point also strongly suggests Wallace was either behind the prank, or a party to it.

Later that evening, one of Jerry Crew's workmates, Jess Bemis, told his wife, Coralie, about the mysterious tracks. Coralie Bemis had a mischievous streak. Over the following days, the pair had some tongue-in-cheek fun spreading evermore-exaggerated gossip about the 'Big Foot' wreaking havoc up at Bluff Creek Road.

Inventing monsters and weird creatures and playing tricks on fellow workers has a long tradition in North American working life. It helped pass the time, and relieved the monotony of routine and backbreaking tasks. Sometimes, the pranks were aimed at young and new workers, as a form of 'hazing' or initiation rite. The legendary figure of Paul Bunyan – a giant lumberjack with supernatural strength and, no doubt, extremely large feet who roamed the woods and forests in the company of his Blue Ox – looms large in the background to these tall tales and mischievous tricks.

Here is one of many examples: in the early years of the twentieth century, a normal-sized lumberjack named Eugene Shepard claimed to have captured and then helped kill what he called a 'hodag'. In spite of its comparatively small stature, when news of it got out, the creature was described as 'the rhino of North America's woods'. A photograph of Shepard and his workmates standing around the dead hodag with axes, rakes and rifles was turned into a postcard, which went on to sell in the hundreds of thousands. But it was all a jape. Shepard and his pals had carved the hodag out of wood, to hoax the general public and for their own amusement. If anything, the made-up creature looks like a cross between a fox, a bull terrier and a pig.

Work continued on the Bluff Creek logging road until the middle of September, when a fresh set of giant tracks appeared.

Viewing these, none of the men was any longer sure that they were part of an elaborate hoax. Even Coralie Bemis, who now heard the men talking about the footprints in awed tones, also began to wonder if a real creature might have left them.

Once he had examined the fresh tracks, Jerry Crew said that if the original footprints had been left as part of an elaborate deception, the new ones looked to him like evidence of an unknown but real creature. One that lived in the forest and came into the camp in the night. One that took a keen interest in any new areas of work that were underway, and occasionally took it into its head to throw large objects around for the heck of it. Anxious to confirm his new belief, Crew made a paper tracing of one of the prints and took it to a taxidermist named Robert Titmus. Titmus had a workshop in the town of Anderson, near Redding, a hundred miles or so south-east of Bluff Creek. Titmus told Crew the tracing lacked the necessary and sufficient detail to be of any use in identifying the mysterious creature, and taught him how to take a plaster cast from a footprint.

Once Crew had done this, he called Titmus again. The taxidermist travelled north with a colleague, Al Corbett, to inspect the cast. The footprint was 18 inches (46cm) long – far bigger than even the most outsized human foot. Even so, Corbett was not impressed, remarking, 'The other workers there at the site have been playing pranks on one another.' Determined to convince them otherwise, Crew gave the visitors a map to the Bluff Creek site, and invited them to go and inspect the tracks for themselves.

While Crew was busy trying to prove his case for the real Big Foot's existence, Coralie Bemis was busy writing a letter detailing the story to Andrew Genzoli, editor of the regional *Humboldt Times* newspaper. Equally unimpressed, Genzoli, like Corbett, suspected that the loggers up at Bluff Creek were playing silly games. As a result, for several days he sat on what was almost certainly the biggest story of his life.

Then, when he had a column to fill on 21 September 1958, Genzoli remembered Coralie's letter. He took it out of the drawer, polished it up a bit and published it. The response from his readers was far more enthusiastic than he had expected. They were agog, and plainly eager for more. Encouraged, Genzoli researched the whole business of the Bluff Creek prints for himself, wrote the story up again from scratch and published it. Enter Betty Allen. A regular *Humboldt Times* correspondent, Mrs Allen was a resident of Willow Creek, a small settlement not far from Bluff Creek. Nowadays, the hamlet describes itself as 'a rugged mountain community nestled in the heart of the Six Rivers National Forest ... located in the Trinity/Shasta/Cascade Region, near the Oregon border, and ... easily reached via State Routes 96 (the 'Bigfoot Scenic Byway') and 299.'

A diligent and thorough journalist, Allen went up to the Bluff Creek camp, talked to the workers, and wrote a few more column inches for Genzoli and the *Humboldt Times*. Together with Genzoli's articles, Allen's journalistic verve and panache helped keep the story alive. Then, on Saturday, 4 October, Jerry Crew visited Genzoli with the plaster cast of the putative Big Foot's foot. The editor let out a whistle. It was way bigger than a human foot, and yet it had toes. Very, very, big toes – which meant that, as Jerry Crew had told him, it could not be the print of a bear. Was there an ancient race of human giants in the forest up there, or was there really some kind of unknown but gigantic non-human creature at large?

Genzoli had a photographer take a picture of Crew examining the cast while he stood looking on. Under the banner headline: 'Huge Footprints Hold Mystery Of Friendly Bluff Creek Giant', the article was printed the next morning in the Sunday edition of the *Humboldt Times*. In it, Genzoli was careful to stress that the creature was friendly: 'the men are often convinced that they are being watched. However, they believe it is not an "unfriendly watching." Nearly every new piece of work . . . finds tracks on it the next morning, as though the thing had a "supervisory interest" in the project. Are the tracks a human hoax? Or, are they the actual marks of a huge but harmless wild-man, traveling [sic] through the wilderness? Can this be some legendary sized animal? Maybe we have a relative of the Abominable Snowman of the Himalayas, our own Wandering Willie of Weitchpec [a hamlet near Bluff Creek] . . .'

In a moment of journalistic brilliance, Genzoli decided that calling the wild creature of the woods 'Bigfoot' rather than 'Big Foot' worked better for the story. It did. The article caught like a bright flame to dry tinder. Genzoli's newly christened 'Bigfoot' exploded onto the international stage. Journalists and reporters from all over the world beat a path to his door, and the idea of a giant, hairy (but ultimately friendly) creature roaming the forests of North America took a firm hold in the popular imagination.

Unfortunately for the many Bigfoot enthusiasts who believed in the Bluff Creek footprints, they turned out to have been faked.

In 2003, Michael Wallace reported that back in 1958 up at Bluff Creek, his father, and Wilbur's brother, Ray L. Wallace, had asked a friend to carve a pair of false wooden feet. He wanted to play a prank on the road-building team. Once he'd taken delivery of them, Ray Wallace had a workmate drive him slowly around the camp, stamping the prints hard into the ground at strategic locations as he went. Wallace had thought the deception through: using a vehicle helped him leave tracks with a gait that was much longer than a bear's.

The exposure may have had a short-term dampening effect on some members of the Bigfoot community. In the long run, though, and in an echo of that other globally famous cryptid, the Loch Ness Monster, Michael Wallace's admission of fakery did nothing to stop the Bigfoot legend from growing. More and more sightings of a 'large, hairy, ape-like creature' loping about in the woods poured into newspapers, radio and television stations. They came not just from the forests of Northern California, but also from woodlands right across the United States and Canada.

One school of thought suggests it was the Coast Salish Native Canadians who originated the Bigfoot story in the first place. Inhabitants of Fraser Valley and Vancouver Island, British Columbia, the Salish had a long tradition of stories that featured a huge, hairy man-monster called the 'Sasquatch'. Similar giant forest cryptids figure in the legends of other Native American tribes. They far pre-date the first reported sighting of strange footprints by an explorer and trader for the Northwest Company named David Thompson. In 1811, Thompson reported finding a set of prints in the snow near what is now the town of Jasper, Alberta. He said they were fourteen inches long and eight inches wide, and that the feet had only four toes. This was very mysterious. Ripples of sensation spread far from the spot.

Thompson's journal entry for 7 January 1811 states: 'I saw the track of a large Animal – has 4 large Toes abt 3 or 4 In [inches] long & a small nail at the end of each. The Bal of his foot sank abt 3 In deeper than his Toes – the hinder part of his foot did not mark well. The whole is about 14 In long by 8 In wide & very much resembles a large Bear's Track. It was in the Rivulet in about 6 In snow.' [Quoted in T.C. Elliott, *Journal of David Thompson*, Oregon Historical Quarterly, 15 (March – June 1914).]

Returning to the experience some 40 years later in *Narrative*, an account of his life and times, Thompson added:

I now recur to what I have already noticed in the early part of last winter, when proceeding up the Athabasca River to cross the mountains, in company with men and four hunters. On one of the channels of the River we came to the track of a large animal, which measured fourteen inches in length by eight inches in breadth by a tape line. As snow was about six inches in depth, the track was well defined and we could see it for a full hundred yards from us. This animal was proceeding from north to south. We did not attempt to follow it, we had not time for it, and the Hunters, eager as they are to follow and shoot every animal, made no attempt to follow this beast, for what could the balls of our fowling guns do against such an animal?

Reports from old times had made the head branches of this River, and the Mountains in the vicinity the abode of one, or more, very large animals, to which I never appeared to give credence. For these reports appeared to arise from that fondness for the marvellous so common to mankind: but the sight of the track of that large a beast staggered me, and I often thought of it, yet never could bring myself to believe such an animal existed, but thought it might be the track of some Monster Bear.

The interesting thing about this account – and a straightforward antidote to all of the hoaxing we looked at above – is that it both rings somewhat true, and is very intriguing. As far as we can tell, Thompson had no interest in creating and circulating a false account of cryptid tracks. Furthermore, he tells us he was reluctant to believe the tracks might be anything other than those of a 'Monster Bear'. This leaves us wondering, what exactly did Thompson see that day, if it wasn't indeed the footprints of an unknown creature?

Whether the legendary nineteenth-century North American circus impresario P.T. Barnum was one of the people who heard about Thompson's sighting of mysterious footprints is not recorded – but in 1846, Barnum exhibited a creature he described as a 'wildman' in his sell-out London show. He claimed the large hairy beast, that ate disgusting food in front of its fascinated audience, had been 'captured in the wilds of California'.

Up until the year 1967, the most persuasive evidence for Bigfoot's existence was the huge number of gigantic footprint reports that poured into news outlets across America. Some of these came with photographs that appear strikingly genuine. Sceptics retort that it is not very difficult to cut a pair of 'Bigfoot Feet' from Styrofoam or some other material, and then tramp around the forest in them at will. Always bear in mind that if you do decide to play this particular trick, a local hunter might see you moving in the dappled shadows, mistake you for fair game and shoot you dead.

On the afternoon of Friday, 20 October 1967, two men named Roger Patterson and Bob Gimlin put a rocket under the whole Bigfoot debate. One-time rodeo workers from Yakima County, Washington, the pair had long been trying to make a docudrama about Bigfoot. In the story they were trying to film, Gimlin, who had Apache heritage, but even so wore a wig for the role, featured as an 'Indian tracker'. An 'old miner' character was also included in an attempt to add authenticity to the yarn.

Patterson had a long-term interest in – not to say, obsession with – the whole subject of Bigfoot. He had already visited the Bluff Creek area more than once, and had published a book the year before entitled *Do Abominable Snowmen of America Really Exist?* Having struggled to get very far with the story and their film, the two men then suddenly got lucky. In fact, if you believe that the 59.5-second, 954-frame footage Patterson shot that autumn day on a rented 16mm camera proves the existence of Bigfoot, the two men got very, very lucky indeed. The clip has become not just internationally famous: it is one of the most-watched pieces of film of all time. It continues to amaze, convince, baffle and incite criticism from viewers all around the world.

Patterson and Gimlin said they were scouting for traces of Bigfoot that afternoon, riding roughly north-east upstream along the east bank of Bluff Creek. Rounding the root system of a huge overturned tree, they saw a large, hairy ape-like creature standing on the opposite bank. Watching them. Patterson says he was only 125 feet (38m) away from the figure when they spotted it. His horse immediately reared up in fright, and it took him about twenty seconds to get it back under control. By that time the creature had turned and begun walking away. Patterson said he grabbed the camera from the saddlebag, ran towards the shambling figure and started filming when he was a stone's throw away from it.

Gimlin says he pulled a rifle from his scabbard in case of trouble, and stood ready to fire. The cryptid walked off into the forest with a lolloping gait. Then, in the most memorable and convincing segment of the whole clip, it turned to look back at Patterson and Gimlin three times. What do we immediately notice? That the creature's arms are very long in proportion to its body; that it has buttocks; a pointy head; female breasts; and that the soles of its feet are noticeably pale.

In a later interview with John Willison Green, a Canadian journalist and leading Bigfoot researcher, Patterson said: 'This creature was on my left, about 125 feet across the creek . . . Its head was very human, though considerably more slanted, and with a large forehead and wide, broad nostrils. Its arms hung almost to its knees when it walked. Its hair was two-to-four inches long, brown underneath, lighter at the top, and covering the entire body except for the face around the nose, mouth and cheek. And it was female; it had big pendulous breasts.'

Patterson and Gimlin's accounts differ on a number of key points.

Patterson first said he thought the creature was between six-and-a-half and seven feet tall. Later, he added a foot to that estimate. Gimlin estimated Bigfoot was about six feet tall.

Ray Wallace, the foreman at the Bluff Creek logging camp later admitted that he had directed Patterson and Gimlin to the spot where Bigfoot happened to appear. The coincidence is remarkable. And maybe a little too pat.

Not that we would want to cast too many aspersions on the story – at least, not as many as Philip Morris, owner of Morris Costumes. In 2002, Mr Morris claimed that he'd sold Patterson the 'ape suit' that was used in the film. When Patterson phoned back to ask how he could 'make the shoulders more massive and the arms longer', Morris says he advised Patterson to insert American football shoulder pads, and hold sticks inside the suit to extend the arms. Another man has claimed he was inside the 'ape suit' that day. None of this troubles Bigfoot stalwarts, who continue to believe the film is incontrovertible proof.

Other sightings report a creature as tall as seven foot ten and weighing in at the best part of a ton. The colour of its fur varies between black, grey, dark reddish-brown and dark chestnut. Several people have said that while they didn't actually see Bigfoot, they got close enough to catch a whiff of its body odour – and that it smelled disgusting. If one ever is caught, a Bigfoot might have a thing or two to say about being described as a giant, malodorous monkey.

Some local authorities have moved to protect Bigfoot. In Skamania County, Washington, where a gang of rampaging Bigfeet reportedly attacked a mining camp, it is illegal to kill a Bigfoot under penalty of a $1,000 fine and five years in jail. The official ordinance declares, 'The Sasquatch, Yeti, Bigfoot, or Giant Hairy Ape are hereby declared to be endangered species of Skamania County, and there is hereby created a Sasquatch refuge . . .' The Sioux Indians, who know it as *'Taku he'*, also forbid Bigfoot hunting on their lands. The hunt for the cryptid nonetheless goes on, not with rifles, but with cameras, binoculars and recording devices.

Despite the many thousands of reports, no one has ever discovered a Bigfoot carcass. The body of a real, uncontested Bigfoot discovered in the forest? Now that would give the non-believers something to think about.

The Green Children of Woolpit

Green children who appear from nowhere? Wearing clothes made of some unknown material, and refusing to eat? It sounds like an early medieval take on a John Wyndham science fiction novel. Yet in the original twelfth-century version, this mysterious tale was presented as a true record of events. Many at the time supposedly saw and spoke to the two youngsters in question.

The story first appears in Book One of William of Newburgh's *Historia rerum Anglicarum,* a history of England between the years 1066 and 1198 that focuses mainly on the lives of the kings (there were no queens during that period). It was picked up and retold by Ralph of Coggeshall in about 1220, and both versions of the tale are written in Latin. Here is Thomas Keightley's 1850 translation of Ralph of Coggeshall's version:

> Another wonderful thing happened in Suffolk, at St. Mary's of the Wolf-pits. A boy and his sister were found by the inhabitants of that place near the mouth of a pit which is there, who had the form of all their limbs like to those of other men, but they differed in the colour of their skin from all the people of our habitable world; for the whole surface of their skin was tinged of a green colour. No one could understand their speech. When they were brought as curiosities to the house of a certain knight, Sir Richard de Calne, at Wikes, they wept bitterly. Bread

153

and other victuals were set before them, but they would touch none of them, though they were tormented by great hunger, as the girl afterwards acknowledged. At length, when some beans just cut, with their stalks, were brought into the house, they made signs, with great avidity, that they should be given to them. When they were brought, they opened the stalks instead of the pods, thinking the beans were in the hollow of them; but not finding them there, they began to weep anew. When those who were present saw this, they opened the pods, and showed them the naked beans. They fed on these with delight, and for a long time tasted no other food. The boy, however, was always languid and depressed, and he died within a short time. The girl enjoyed continual good health; and becoming accustomed to various kinds of food, lost completely that green colour, and gradually recovered the sanguine habit of her entire body. She was afterwards regenerated by means of holy baptism, and lived for many years in the service of that knight (as I have frequently heard from him and his family), and was rather loose and wanton in her conduct. Being frequently asked about the people of her country, she asserted that the inhabitants, and all they had in that country, were of a green colour; and that they saw no sun, but enjoyed a degree of light like what is after sunset. Being asked how she came into this country with the aforesaid boy, she replied, that as they were following their flocks, they came to a certain cavern, on entering which they heard a delightful sound of bells; ravished by whose sweetness, they went for a long time wandering on through the cavern, until they came to its mouth. When they came out of it, the excessive light of the sun, and the unusual temperature of the air struck them senseless; and they thus lay for a long time. Being terrified by the noise of those who came on them, they wished to fly, but they could not find the entrance of the cavern before they were caught.

William of Newbridge or Newburgh, or Newbury places the

story in the reign of King Stephen. He says he long hesitated to believe it, but he was at length overcome by the weight of evidence. According to William, the place where the children appeared was about four or five miles from Bury St. Edmund's: they came in harvest-time out of the Wolf-pits; they both lost their green hue, and were baptised and learned English. The boy, who was the younger, died; but the girl married a man at Lenna, and lived many years. They said their country was called St. Martin's Land, as that saint was chiefly worshiped there; that the people were Christians, and had churches; that the sun did not rise there, but that there was a bright country which could be seen from theirs, being divided from it by a very broad river.

A few lines give us a flavour of Ralph's original manuscript:

De quodam puero et puella de terra emergentibus. Aliud quoque mirum priori non dissimile in Suthfolke contigit apud Sanctam Mariam de Wulpetes. In ventus est puer quidam cum sorore sua ab accolis loci illius juxta oram cujusdam foveae quse ibidem continetur, qui formam omnium membrorum cseteris hominibus similem habebant, sed in colore cutis ab omnibus mortalibus nostrae habitabilis discrepabant. Nam tota superficies cutis eorum viridi colore tingebatur. Loquelam eorum nullus intelligere potuit. Hic igitur ad CHRONICON ANGLICANUM. 119

Fun, no?

William, who was a canon at the Augustinian priory of Newburgh, Yorkshire, was born in Bridlington in that same most beautiful and expansive county. He seems to have lived out his life there, straying rarely. His *History of English Affairs* covers the period 1066–1198, and, at the same time as giving us some idea of what the post-Norman monarchs and their more or less murderous barons were up to – for the most part, it appears they were fighting among themselves, visiting every shade of chaos on the local population, and using violence against anyone who disagreed with them – the book provides a fascinating insight into twelfth-century English medieval life. Besides *The Green Children of Woolpit*, it includes many other weird and wonderful tales. Since one of William's interests was revenants, his text also contains one of the earliest, if not the very first, British mentions of vampires.

Written at the behest of Ernald, bishop of Rievaulx Abbey, William's story, while broadly similar to Ralph's, varies in some of its details. The children are still green in colour, but they are discovered by harvesters when they emerge from one of the *wulf-pyttes*, or wolf-pits that were dotted around the village to protect livestock and locals from the ravenous beasts that apparently preyed on them in those days, and which gave the settlement its name. The children are also wearing strangely coloured clothes made of some unknown material.

The farm hands take the pair to the village, where everyone flocks to see them but where, despite being half-dead from starvation, they refuse to touch any of the food the villagers offer them. But when they catch sight of a basket of green beans, the more-or-less identically hued children grab these health-giving vegetables and gobble them down.

After many weeks on a strict, self-imposed and chlorophyll-rich vegan diet, which just about kills them, the interlopers learn to eat bread and other foods – whereupon they lose their green pigmentation, learn English, and are confessed into the Christian religion. Despite this act of potential salvation, the boy shortly dies. The girl, though, not only becomes just like any other woman in the region, she marries a man from the village of Lynn, and when the story ends, William tells us she is still alive.

The villagers of Woolpit were luckier than the inhabitants of Midwich in John Wyndham's novel *The Midwich Cuckoos*. Filmed in 1960 by German director Wolf Rilla as *Village of the Damned*, and then remade by John Carpenter in 1995, it featured children with paranormal powers. Among these is the ability to read the minds of the benighted villagers, and force them to do things against their will. The poster for the movie warns us to 'Beware The Stare That Will Paralyze The Will Of The World'. Before they are eventually defeated, the staring children indulge in a spot of casual murder, and show promising signs of being able to take over the entire human race. Luckily, a professor manages to block their mind-reading powers for just long enough to detonate a time bomb, and put paid to the evil little blighters for good.

The story of the Green Children may strike some other distant narrative chords: one is the Old English folk-tale of Jack and the Beanstalk, which irrepressible plant the young hero climbs to cross from this world into another – a reversal of the Green Children/St Martin's Land direction of travel. Then there is the fact that, in one version of the story, the Green Children are discovered near the mouth of a wolf-pit, hinting at the idea that, as in the legend of Romulus and Remus, they were raised by wolves. Going even further out on the story limb and beginning to saw, we can speculate that the children reached the surface of the Earth from an entirely hidden, subterranean world à la Jules Verne.

The son of a Roman cavalry officer, St Martin, who lived roughly between AD 316 and 397, renounced both his father's example and a military career to become a stalwart of the early Christian church. Even today, children in some parts of Flanders, the Netherlands, Austria and Germany celebrate St Martin's Day by making and processing with paper lanterns, and singing songs to his greater glory. This suggests a long-standing association between the saint and the young whose origins and import may now be lost to us, but might just bear on the Green Children's claim to have come from 'St Martin's Land'.

And finally: little green beings who don't speak our language or eat the same food, except for the greenest, skinniest vegetable they can find; who came through a long tunnel, following enchanting sounds; and who wear clothes made from unknown materials? Does this lead us to conclude that 'St Martin's Land', then, is actually – Mars? Or that the Green Children came to Earth from a parallel universe, via a wormhole in space-time?

The Phaistos Disc

It must be a strange feeling to hold the key to an ancient civilisation in your hands and not be able to use it. This, apparently, was what Italian archaeologist Luigi Pernier experienced on 3 July 1908, when he found the Phaistos Disc. It came to light in a basement room of the ruined Minoan palace of Phaistos, near present-day Hagia Triada on the south coast of Crete. Or did it?

One of the most controversial objects in the history of archaeology, the Phaistos Disc is also one of its longest-standing mysteries. Over the years, dozens of professional and amateur sleuths have attempted to decipher the script's exact meaning – if it is a script – but to date there is no universally accepted solution.

Each side of the fired clay disc has a set of mysterious symbols stamped into it. These number 242 in total, and most scholars agree that they run in a spiral sequence from its edges towards the centre. That is about all they do agree on. In all, there are 45 different symbols, but no one is sure whether its Minoan creator meant them to be read in a clockwise or an anti-clockwise direction.

Many of the pictographs or glyphs portray recognisable objects. These include: a human figure with a startling 'Mohican' hairstyle, like an ancient punk rocker of the kind Britain witnessed in the 1970s; a boat; a child; different kinds of birds;

some fish; various insects and plants; a woman, or goddess; and a number of weapons. In addition, 18 thin, incised lines appear to divide the character or symbol groups into what might be separate words or phrases. There are also faint traces of corrections made by the creator or scribe.

Tentatively dated to between 1950 and 1400 BC – although archaeologists disagree even about this – the fired clay disc is about 16 centimetres in diameter and one centimetre thick. This is probably a bit too small for it to have been a board game, which is one of the more inventive suggestions for its possible use. It was, though, clearly portable, suggesting it might have been of use in different locations.

Explanations for what the symbols might signify as a whole include: a flood narrative; a royal genealogy; a calendar; a sea shanty (at least on one side); a hymn to a pregnant Minoan goddess; the account of a battle; a curse; a message from King Nestor sorting out a Cretan territorial dispute; and many, many more besides.

The Minoan civilisation was truly remarkable. Centred on the island of Crete, it flourished during the Middle Bronze Age from about 2600–1100 BC, establishing a trading empire that came to dominate much if not all of the Aegean area. Its two most famous sites, Knossos and Phaistos, are among the greatest archaeological treasures ever discovered. The existence of a brilliant civilisation predating – and in many ways, outstripping – the better-known Troy only came to light in 1900, when British archaeologist Sir Arthur Evans hired a small army of local diggers, and began excavating a flower-covered hill at Knossos, a few miles to the south-east of present-day Heraklion.

Some archaeologists believe the fact that no other objects featuring the same set of symbols have ever been found means that the disc is an elaborate hoax, or a forgery. They accuse Pernier of fabricating it to boost his reputation. Establishing its date of manufacture by means of thermo luminescence would help confirm the disc's authenticity, but citing the disc's fragility, the Heraklion Archaeological Museum, where it is currently on display, has so far refused all requests to allow this.

The fact that the symbols on the disc were stamped into the clay with a system of durable, high-quality and reusable matrices means that, if authentic, the Phaistos Disc embodies the world's earliest known example of movable type – and one that was invented some 2,800 years before Gutenberg's 1439 printing press helped bring light to the world. Given this, forging the disc would have been a Herculean task: each tiny symbol would have to have been individually hand-carved onto the end of a separate punch, before being stamped into the fresh clay.

A fired clay tablet known as 'PH-1' unearthed a few inches away from the Phaistos Disc may have left us a small clue to its meaning. It was marked with the first known example of the ancient Minoan language known as 'Linear A', which some experts believe is closely related to the inscription on the disc. Others disagree entirely with this interpretation.

Many of the attempts that have been made to decipher the disc and its unique inventory of symbols link it to other ancient languages, such as Proto-Greek, Anatolian, Semitic, and even early Polynesian.

More radical theories claim the disc is a message from extra-terrestrial beings, or that it acts as a portal or 'stargate' that enables humans – presumably by means of a wormhole – to travel through space-time. Once, that is, they have learned how to use it. The jury is still out on that one, too.

At Knossos, Arthur Evans and his team uncovered a vast labyrinth of hundreds of interconnecting rooms. He promptly dubbed it the Palace of Minos. In fact, the site may have been a complex used by the surrounding population as a place of religious and sacred ritual. Its other possible uses have not been fully established. Whatever its purpose, even today Knossos is a wonderful place. A series of highly colourful and striking murals give the modern visitor a direct insight into what life was like in the complex some four thousand years ago. The vibrant images of strikingly-dressed, bare-breasted priestesses, young boys boxing and bull-jumping to prove their mettle, women in what looks very much like an early version of the bikini, dolphins gambolling in the waves and many other visual wonders give the strong impression of a society with a rich, stable, happy and vibrant culture. The only note of caution to sound here is that the Swiss artists Evans employed to 'repaint' some of the murals may also have done more than just join the dots. Many of the artefacts found at the site were only reassembled following many hours of painstaking work. As long as you don't object to this kind of restoration – and many professional archaeologists now do – the effort paid off, leaving us a legacy of wonders.

One of the first items to be unearthed was a bull-headed *rhyton*, or vessel for offering libations to the gods. Charged with latent meaning and power, it defies us to look away. The many images of bulls painted on the walls of Knossos, and its labyrinthine character, inspired Evans to name the civilisation he had newly discovered after the Ancient Greek mythological King Minos. The son of Zeus and Europa and first king of Crete, every nine years Minos made the Athenian King Aegeus send seven young men and seven young women drawn by lots into the heart of the labyrinth beneath the palace. Here, in the shadowed, mazy chambers, lurked the legendary half-man, half-bull monster we know as the Minotaur. At home in the darkness, it slaughtered and devoured the sacrificial victims.

For many years, no one knew how to defeat the monster. At last, King Minos's daughter, Ariadne, fell in love with the hero Theseus, and helped him navigate the maze. He met and killed the Minotaur, rescued the latest batch of innocents, and made his way back out thanks to Ariadne's cunning and a ball of string.

A major earthquake destroyed both the earlier palace of Phaistos and the complex at Knossos around 1628 BC. This may have been caused by a volcanic eruption on the nearby island of Thera/Santorini. Other Minoan sites suffered catastrophic damage at the same time. Knossos itself is thought to have been at least partially rebuilt towards the end of the Later Bronze Age.

The symbols found on two other intriguing finds may link them to the Phaistos Disc. The first is a votive double axe or *labrys* found by Spyridon Marinatos in the Arkalohori Cave, Crete. The second is a fragment of a much smaller clay disc, excavated at Vladikavkaz, in North Ossetia. Unlike the Phaistos Disc, these artefacts were engraved and not impressed. The Vladikavkaz disc has mysteriously disappeared from the archaeological record.

The Cat in the Box

'I cannot seriously believe in quantum theory because it cannot be reconciled with the idea that physics should represent a reality in time and space, free from spooky actions at a distance.'

Albert Einstein, March 1947

In the beginning there was the light, and for centuries light was thought to travel in waves. And it does. But then early in the twentieth century, two of the most important physicists in history, Albert Einstein and Max Planck, realised that light also travels in tiny individual packets of energy known as 'quanta' (from the Latin *quantum*, an amount), which cannot be broken down into smaller particles. In the case of light, these nano-particles are known as photons.

During the same period of intense and revolutionary scientific advancement, physicists also discovered that sub-atomic particles like photons and electrons enjoy 'wave-particle duality' – which is to say that they can behave either as a particle, or as a wave. Which is very odd. Odder still, the state that sub-atomic particles 'choose' to adopt depends on whether they are, or are not, being observed. This behaviour, which also holds true for electrons, atoms and even whole molecules, was a very unsettling thing to discover in the early part of the twentieth century. It remains very unsettling today.

To find out more about the 'spooky' behaviour of these nano-particles, physicists conducted a series of groundbreaking experiments. Among these, the 'double slit experiment' must count as one of the most intellectually shocking and significant ever devised, in that it challenges the fundamental nature of what we previously understood as our physical reality. The double-slit experiment was designed to tell us where a given fundamental particle – an electron, a photon, or whatever – is at any given moment, and what it is doing. It tells us exactly the opposite.

In the double-slit experiment, an electron gun – let's use electrons for now – fires a stream of individual electrons at two identical, vertical slits cut in a plate of some solid material. A photosensitive screen that can detect and register any electrons passing through the slits is placed behind the plate.

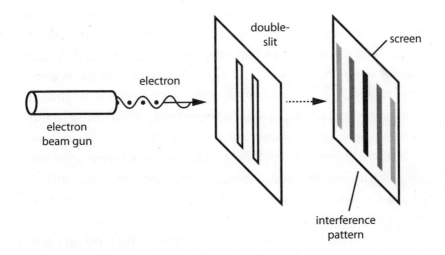

The Double-slit Experiment

According to the laws of classical physics, each electron should choose one or other of the slits to go through more or less at random, and in more or less equal numbers. When enough particles have done this, they should appear on the receptor screen as roughly vertical lines, one in line with each slit. So far, so good. But against all expectations, they don't. Instead, the electrons form an interference pattern on the screen that is typical of a wave. It's as if each individual electron had somehow travelled through both slits at the same time, and then, in mysterious teamwork with all the other individual electrons, had decided to behave as a wave. This is weird, and runs counter to all the accepted rules of what is often called classical, or Newtonian physics. It gets stranger and less reasonable still when you learn that, time after time, in experiment after experiment, the electrons only decide to act as a wave *when they are not being watched*. Not only that, but a recent experiment suggests that the degree of particle misbehaviour is in direct proportion to the degree of observation.

In an effort to find out why the electrons and other sub-atomic particles were behaving in this extraordinary way, researchers placed detectors next to the slits, hoping to catch particles in the act of going through one slit or another – or both at the same time. As soon as they did this, the individual particles stopped behaving as a wave and went back to behaving as well-behaved streams, forming nice, predictable vertical patterns in line with the slits. Switch the detectors off again, and hey, presto! the electrons immediately took on the characteristics of a wave, and the classically unaccountable wave interference pattern reappeared.

To the astonished scientists, the electrons seemed to be behaving like naughty schoolchildren. Not only that, they had a hive mind. They were communicating, interacting or 'interfering' with one another to behave collectively as a wave when they were not being measured – and then splitting up to act as if everything was normal when they were.

This odd and apparently secretive behaviour, which apparently holds true for all subatomic particles everywhere in the known universe, undermines a great deal of what physicists previously thought they understood about the nature of reality and existence. In classical physics, matter is fixed and certain and not liable to change from one state to another at any given instant, depending on whether or not someone is watching it.

In an attempt to provide an explanation for the 'observer effect' or double slit phenomenon, the eminent physicists Niels Bohr and Werner Heisenberg came up with the 'Copenhagen Interpretation' of quantum behaviour. This proposes that a given particle has no actual physical properties whatsoever, and exists only as a quantum 'wave function' that encapsulates all of its possible final states and locations all of the time – unless and until it is subjected to observational experiment. The term 'superposition' was coined as a shorthand way of describing this inherently uncertain and unstable state of quantum particles. Bohr, Heisenberg and others proposed that the quantum state of any given subatomic particle 'collapses' into a single end state when it is observed, in some way deciding to behave either as a wave, or as a particle.

Heisenberg's Uncertainty Principle takes us a little further into the existential mire. It proposes that the location and momentum (the mass times speed) of a particle are complementary variables: the more we know about one property, the less we can know about the other – to the point where if a particle's location becomes certain, its momentum becomes unknowable, and vice versa.

Spooky indeed. Does all of this mean that the universe is continually obliging particles to choose between two different states of being? Does it imply that, if we know its momentum, we cannot be sure of a particle's location at any given time? The short answer, if you adhere to quantum theory as an accurate description of matter, is 'yes'.

How about the idea that every time a particle 'chooses' a final, 'collapsed' state, the universe splits, and a new one is formed? According to the 'many worlds' theory, this is exactly what does happen, not just once, but on and on, *ad infinitum*, to the last syllable of (un)recorded time. What, then, are the implications for other, somewhat larger, or macroscopic states of matter in the galaxy like ourselves? Are we humans continually switching between realities without realising it, as a function of some conscious or unconscious choice? Or does our sheer relative size and mass somehow preclude that?

Common sense tells us that we are not continually shifting states, but we all know the feeling that, if only we had made a certain choice at a certain time – gone back into the carriage before the doors closed, and talked to the person inside who had shown reciprocal interest – then our lives might have been fundamentally different. Or does that belong in a different category of existential choice?

When it was first proposed, quantum theory upset a great many scientists. Most prominent among the dissenters from the 'uncertainty' or 'probabilistic' view of things was Albert Einstein, who famously said: 'God does not play dice.' The exact quote, in a letter to fellow-scientist and quantum theorist Max Born states: 'In our scientific expectations we have progressed towards antipodes. You believe in the dice-playing God, and I in complete law and order in a world which objectively exists, and which I, in a wildly speculative way, am trying to capture . . . Even the great initial success of quantum theory does not make me believe in the fundamental dice game.'

Instead, in his theory of 'local realism', Einstein argued that particles must have a pre-existing, 'real' value before any possible measurement is made that throws doubt on their physical state. However, quantum experimentation since then – and even at the time – appears consistently to disprove this pragmatic view of things.

In 1935, in another attempt to disprove the notion that fundamental particles and so everything else in the universe – including ourselves – exist as a fog of 'hesitant' particles, Einstein's contemporary and fellow quantum-dissenter Erwin Schrödinger came up with a famous thought-experiment. Known as 'Schrödinger's Cat', this little beauty really does stretch the grey matter.

Here is Schrödinger's original text: 'one can even set up quite ridiculous cases. A cat is penned up in a steel chamber, along with the following device (which must be secured against direct interference by the cat): in a Geiger counter, there is a tiny bit of radioactive matter, so small, that perhaps in the course of the hour one of the atoms decays, but also, with equal probability, perhaps none; if it happens, the counter tube discharges and through a relay releases a hammer that shatters a small flask of hydrocyanic acid. If one has left this entire system to itself for an hour, one would say that the cat still lives if meanwhile no atom has decayed. The first atomic decay would have poisoned it. The psi-function of the entire system would express this by having in it the living and dead cat (pardon the expression) mixed or smeared out in equal parts.'

In accordance with the laws of quantum mechanics, Schrödinger's 'tiny bit of radioactive matter' has the constant potential to decay and release a high-energy particle, or not. If the decay occurs, the Geiger counter detects the particle. This triggers the hammer, which smashes the flask, which releases the poison and kills the cat. If there is no radioactive decay and thus no particle release, the cat does not die.

The Copenhagen Interpretation states that the atom in question is in a superposition, or state of multiple possibilities, and so might or might not decay, unless and until we observe it. But – and in science, there's almost always a 'but' – we are not supposed to look inside. The moment we raise the lid of the box and take a peek, the atom will 'know' it is being observed. Its superposition will collapse, it will choose a final state, and the cat will either die or it will keep right on purring. But until we do that, the cat, like the atom, will theoretically remain in an indeterminate state.

How can this possibly be? Since the question was first posed, many physicists propose that 'somehow' the radioactive atom in the box is 'observed' and that this decides its final or end state. What nobody can convincingly explain is how this actually happens. Does the Geiger counter in the box itself constitute a form of observation that the atom somehow detects? That's one theory. Another is that, in accordance with the 'many worlds' theory, the cat remains both dead and alive regardless of whether or not it is being observed – i.e., it occupies the two possible end states simultaneously, either in different branches of our own universe, or in different universes. There have been many other theoretical attempts to resolve or explain Erwin Schrödinger's famous paradox, but so far none has found universal acceptance.

As if all of this were not enough to make us dizzy, quantum mechanics gets even more bizarre when we consider a couple of other things it throws up. The first of these is 'quantum fluctuation'. Touching once again on Heisenberg's Uncertainty Principle, if we use the rules of his equation, but substitute energy and time for momentum and location, we find that the shorter the lifespan of a given particle, the less certain we can be about its energy.

This leads on logically to a very strange result: always provided they exist for an almost infinitesimally short space of time, it is theoretically possible that particles can and do 'pop' into existence from nothing. The spontaneous generation of these 'virtual particles' appears once again to violate all the rules of classical physics, not to mention common sense.

An experiment called 'The Casimir Effect' appears to confirm the existence of these virtual particles. In quantum field
theory, a vacuum, far from being 'empty' – i.e., entirely devoid
of energy or particles in the classical sense – is in reality filled
with fluctuating electromagnetic waves. When two metal plates,
or mirrors, are placed a few nanometers apart, the smaller
waves will still fit between these twin surfaces; but the longer
electromagnetic waves will not. As a result, there is a tiny bit
less energy in the space between the plates than there is in the
vacuum surrounding them. And as a result of that, the plates
are attracted to one another, proving the existence of the virtual
'pop-up' particles.

The further idea that the vacuum energy observed in the
Casimir effect may be infinite, when calculated in quantum
field terms, suggests that the 'vacuum' of space could in fact be
a source of infinite energy. Known as 'zero point energy', this
further contradicts Einstein's theory of gravitation.

These and other experiments may mean that space, which
we think of as empty, is not in fact empty at all: instead, there
are billions of virtual particles popping in and out of existence
everywhere all the time. Physicists call this theoretical activity
'quantum foam'. Is this ever-simmering cauldron of quantum
possibilities flickering in and out of existence the missing 'dark
matter' that cosmologists have been seeking for so long? Does
it help to explain the very beginning of our universe, the instant
known as the 'Big Bang'? Probably not, in either case. But as
time goes on, the number of unsolved mysteries quantum theory
throws up only increases: not least, the issue of whether or not
there is chronological time as we human beings understand it.

Finally, and before going to lie down in a darkened room, we
should take a sideswipe at 'quantum entanglement'. According
to this theory, subatomic particles that are 'paired' – i.e., exist in
interdependent quantum states – 'know' when a measurement

The Book of Unexplained Mysteries

has been performed on one or other of them, even when, as in the case of the double-slit experiment, there is no means by which, at least in terms of classical physics, the particles can possibly be communicating one with another.

As soon as a measurement is taken of one entangled particle, and it adopts a single 'collapsed' quantum state, its partner adopts the opposite state. Now for the really exciting bit: experimentation seems to prove that this happens *regardless of the distance between the entangled particles*. So, if one particle is at one end of the universe, and one at the other, the corresponding transformation happens faster than the speed of light. If this is true, it means that when viewed in quantum terms, our own sense of strict, chronological time is almost literally meaningless. It exists only as a function of our own personal memories and future projections. Instead, all matter exists in all possible states of being and time, in perpetuity. No wonder Einstein, who was convinced that nothing could possibly travel faster than light, and believed that he had proved it scientifically, did his best to challenge and circumvent so much of quantum theory.

One day, thanks to quantum physics, we may be able to avoid traffic jams by teleporting ourselves across great distances, and travel backwards and forwards in what we know as time. We will own computers that work so efficiently and fast that, by clicking our fingers like Mary Poppins, our wishes will come true. In the meantime, you may very well like me still be wondering – what the devil happened to the cat in the box?

172

The Wow! Signal

In *The Hitchhiker's Guide to the Galaxy*, Douglas Adams told us he had discovered 'The Ultimate Answer to Life, The Universe and Everything . . .' It was '42'! This may be funny, but it doesn't satisfy the desire to understand why we are here, what life might mean and whether the universe exploded randomly into being, or was created by some unseen hand. There is also the small matter of whether, as conscious and sentient beings, we are alone in the whirling corridors of space and time.

Finding an answer to that last mystery might very well help us gain insight to the others. If we did discover and manage to communicate with extraterrestrial life, then its – or perhaps their – view of reality and space-time would almost certainly help shed light on our own. Unless that alien life is both lethally hostile and technologically superior – in which case we won't have to worry: à la H.G. Wells, giant, mechanical three-legged monsters will hunt us down and blast us to smithereens with their death rays.

In the meantime, we keep right on looking for answers to the big questions. The amount of money, effort and drive that goes into detecting evidence of life beyond Earth is astounding. Known as SETI, the Search for Extraterrestrial Intelligence has been going on for a surprisingly long time. In 1869, the physicist, engineer, inventor and futurist Nikola Tesla conducted a series of experiments at his Colorado Springs lab with a view to contacting 'beings' on Mars. A few weeks later, Tesla informed an astonished world that he had indeed made contact with life on the red planet. His instruments had detected an unexplained, repeating signal that seemed to stop transmitting whenever Mars set in the night sky. No unchallenged scientific proof of this contact was ever established; but from that moment on, the quest for life in our home galaxy and beyond began to accelerate.

One of the greatest mysteries about life on Earth is the fact that our planet supports it in the first place. Sometimes called the 'Goldilocks planet', Earth has either been extremely lucky – or, some argue, extremely well designed – to support the creation and persistence of its myriad life forms.

In 1957, work started on a giant radio telescope equipped with a vast parabolic reflector. Nicknamed 'The Big Ear', the Ohio State University Radio Observatory telescope began the world's first continuous Search for Extraterrestrial Intelligence. Nothing of any significance was detected for the best part of 20 years. Then, on 15 August 1977, a volunteer named Jerry Ehman witnessed the most thrilling breakthrough to date in the search for extraterrestrial intelligence. Reviewing data that The Big Ear had detected a few days previously, Ehman spotted evidence of an extremely strong, unexplained signal from the constellation Sagittarius. Someone out there had apparently fired a 72-second, narrowband radio transmission into the void. It was an unmodulated, continuous wave signal. That means it could not contain a 'message', in the sense that we understand it. Even so, the signal bore all the expected hallmarks of extraterrestrial origin – and could not be otherwise explained. Big Ear's systems faithfully recorded the transmission in the form of an alphanumeric code – '6EQUJ5' – where each character represents a sample of the signal taken every 12 seconds. Delighted and amazed, Ehman circled the encoded transmission on the printout in red ink, wrote 'Wow!' next to it, and changed history.

Many people think 'The Wow! Signal', as it became known, still constitutes the best – and only – truly scientific evidence for the existence of extraterrestrial life. Many subsequent attempts were made to find other transmissions from the same quadrant of the sky, but none has ever proved successful. So the mystery of who – or what – might have produced the Wow! signal persists.

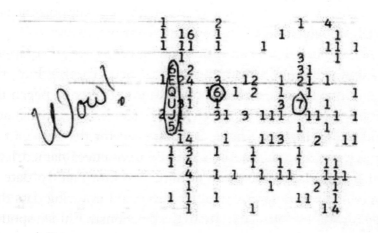

Now, two new SETI projects are aiming to make a new breakthrough. The first, dubbed 'Breakthough Listen', got underway in 2017. It will conduct searches using the Parkes Observatory in New South Wales, Australia, and the Green Bank Telescope in West Virginia, USA. The project will scan frequency ranges between 500 MHz and 15 GHz simultaneously, processing any promising results with more computing power than has ever previously been applied to the quest. And it won't just focus on the Milky Way – it will also be listening for signs of life in the next *one hundred* nearest galaxies to our own.

The second hunt for extraterrestrial life sounds almost too much like a science fiction script to be true. In April 2018, billionaire philanthropist and inventor Elon Musk's SpaceX Company launched a planet-hunting satellite the size of a large refrigerator into orbit for the US National Aeronautics and Space Administration (NASA). Once it reaches its final orbit, the Transiting Exoplanet Survey Satellite – more charmingly known as TESS – will begin searching the galaxy with special cameras and new, high-tech instrumentation for 'exoplanets' that might support life. Could it find the kind of life we know on Earth? Or a form that is entirely different, and that we can barely understand? TESS is going to be up there for a couple of years, doing its best to find out whether we have any neighbours.

How will TESS's instruments do that? An exoplanet is 'a planet outside our own solar system that orbits another star'. When one of these planets passes in front of its home star, it briefly dims that sun's light, creating a detectable 'blink'. TESS carries extraordinary new 'Darkness' cameras that filter out much of the home star's background light that would otherwise overwhelm the planetary information. These telltale twinkles not only tell scientists the size of the planet in question, but how long it takes to complete its orbit – plus a few other things.

Space-based instruments like the new James Webb Space Telescope can then analyse factors like the composition of the planet's atmosphere; its mass; to what degree it is rocky, like Earth, or gassy, like Neptune; how hot it is – and most important of all, whether there is evidence of an alien metabolism living in its environment. The analysis of gas emissions may be a key indicator of intelligent alien activity (although the opposite is true in humans). On Earth, the continuing destruction of climate-regulating rainforest, and the rise in greenhouse gas emissions that goes with it, suggests a form of life that has some way to go before it can be truly described as 'intelligent'.

TESS is picking up the challenge from NASA's previous SETI bloodhound, Kepler, which has been running since 2009. Unlike Kepler, which only scanned a small segment of the sky, TESS will be investigating a massive 85 per cent of the visible universe. Kepler did a great initial job, finding more than 2,300 exoplanets in the relatively small patch of space it was searching. But most of these were too far away; too hot; too cold; lacked water; and orbited stars that were too dim. So, not quite Goldilocks enough.

If it works as planned, TESS will change all that. Her instruments will scan almost all of the stars we can see with the naked eye on a nice, dark night – and several hundred thousand more that are relatively close. (The distances are astonishing: in this case, 'close' means within 300 or so light years of Earth.) Better still, TESS will home in much more successfully than Kepler on stars that show the conditions likely to support some form of intelligent life as we understand the term.

We've had lots of false starts in the search for extraterrestrial intelligence, and quite a few hoaxes. There have also been simple misunderstandings: the strange humanoid figures some claim to have seen in Roswell Air Force Base were very likely parachute test dummies. Released from high altitude balloons, the lifelike mannequins were dropped from varying heights to find out what happens to the human form under the extreme stress conditions of High-Altitude, High-Opening (HAHO) or High-Altitude, Low-Opening (HALO) parachute jumps. These trials took place over a number of decades beginning in the 1950s. Not all of the test dummies were recovered from whichever barren tract of desert they happened to land in.

Laid out for subsequent inspection in the Roswell research

labs, some of these dummies may have prompted the fake 'alien autopsy' video that helped fuel conspiracy theories. It might also explain other reports of alien life in the base. Thankfully, since we still have more questions than answers about the universe and our place in it, none of these false trails and setbacks has stopped SETI.

The list of Goldilocks factors that helped Earth become a planet that supports life is miraculously – and mysteriously – long. We are at just the right distance from our sun for our surface water to remain liquid; the Earth's magnetic field protects us from harmful extraneous forces like solar flares; our sun is just the right size to remain in a stable state for billions of years; we have the perfect atmospheric pressure to sustain human life; and our nice, big moon helps stabilise the 'axial wobble' that might otherwise cause much more extreme and frequent fluctuations in climate. The moon also gives us the ebb and flow of the tides, slowing the Earth's rotation to a happy 24 hours a day, and we have a protective ozone layer that blocks otherwise incoming radiation.

There are many, many more factors that go to make up the Goldilocks phenomenon – so many, and part of so intricate a pattern that some reckon the chances of them all combining in one ecstatic happenstance are so great they must indicate the hand of a divine creator. Others, including many scientists, counter that the universe is so amazingly vast and in so great a state of continual flux that the chance and extremely fortunate combination of positive factors we enjoy is no more than statistically probable, and did flourish in the case of Earth, luckily for us.

Which brings us back to the greatest unsolved mystery of human life: is the answer '42', or do we have company in deep space? Researchers at the La Silla Observatory in Chile are also trying to help us find out. Using the European Southern

Observatory's High Accuracy Radial Velocity Planet Searcher (HARPS), they recently discovered a planet with the conditions to support life. Known as Ross 128 b, it orbits a red dwarf star. The planet is moving ever nearer to Earth. Already a (mere!) eleven light years away, in 80,000 years from now Ross 128 b will become our nearest neighbour, knocking our current next-door planet, Proxima b, off its perch.

Although it is very close to its parent star, Ross 128 b enjoys a relatively temperate climate, ranging from –60 to 20°C (–76 to 68°F). If there is enough water on Ross 128 b to support animal and human life, then we may just have company.

The most electrifying hint that extraterrestrial life may really exist is very recent. In January 2019, a team of scientists at the Canadian Hydrogen Intensity Mapping Experiment (CHIME) in British Columbia announced a 'cosmic flash'. They had detected a second series of Fast Radio Bursts (FRBs) that are set on 'repeat'. The bursts – or 'transmissions' – emanate from a fixed single location in deep space.

Astronomers and alien hunters are both mystified and excited by the fact that these repeating signals have now been detected not once, but twice. They appear all over the sky, and astronomers do not know what causes them.

The first repeating FRBs were detected in 2015 at the Arecibo Observatory in Puerto Rico, with its famous 1,000ft single aperture telescope. The new series came from a separate, but equally precise location far beyond our own galaxy, at a distance of some 1.6 billion light years from Earth.

The CHIME array was originally designed to explore the early universe. Unlike a conventional, upright dish radio telescope, it consists of a series of long, low, semi-cylindrical trough-like structures.

The fact that some of the radio bursts are low frequency deepens the mystery, as it rules out some of the scientific models that had been put forward to explain their origin. The CHIME astronomers have also excluded cataclysmic events as the source of the bursts. So what – or who – is causing them?

We don't yet know enough about space, time and matter to understand our place in what Buzz Lightyear called 'infinity and beyond!' but the impulse to go on trying is irresistible. We want explanations for the ultimate mysteries, and we're not going to stop until we get them.

The Rising Star Cave

Did Gollum really exist? The sinister, lamp-eyed goblin-hunter of J.R.R. Tolkien's fantasy novel *The Hobbit* is the brilliant invention of a great writer's imagination; and yet, the discovery of an entirely new human-like species in the remote and profound darkness of the Dinaledi (Rising Star) cave complex sounds some strange echoes with Tolkien's character.

The Rising Star caves lie some 50km (31 miles) north-east of Johannesburg, South Africa, in the Cradle of Humankind World Heritage Site. And when it comes to investigating them, size matters. The difficulty modern humans have in moving through the maze of crevices, chutes and passageways already gives us an insight into the build of the early hominins who used it.

A number of strong, wiry and intrepid women were recruited to help rewrite the story of early human development. To be fair, there is the odd man in the mix – it was a pair of male South African speliologists who first discovered, and then had the nerve to enter, the extremely small keyhole fissure that gives access in the first place. But many of the subsequent passageways are so low – 25.4cm (10in) high – and so narrow – 18cm (7in) wide – that all bar the slenderest of male cavers tend to get stuck.

Never mind the cramped conditions – it's what the explorers found inside a tiny space dubbed the 'Dinaledi Chamber' (the

Chamber of Stars) that is changing our view of our ancient past. Led by palaeoanthropologist Professor Lee Berger of Witwatersrand University, the team came upon the discovery of their dreams: more than 1,550 fossilised bones. They were the remains of an entirely unknown hybrid human-like species – one that would force scientists to recalibrate their entire understanding of early human development. Naming the new species *Homo naledi* – literally 'Star human' or 'Starman' – '*naledi*' means 'star' in the Sotho language – the experts painstakingly excavated and then documented the bones. They include the remains of at least 15 separate individuals of both sexes, and range in age from infants to elderly adults. They have been reliably dated to between 236,000 and 335,000 years ago.

Standing no more than 152cm (5ft) tall and weighing in at an average 45kg (7 stone), an adult *H. naledi* had a brain the size of an orange; yet its build betrayed a remarkable combination of both human and non-human traits, and the brain formation much more resembles our own than it does other early species such as *Homo heidelbergensis*. This means that *H. naledi* might well have possessed speech, and been able to make tools.

From the waist down, this petite ancient cousin's physique was a great deal like our own, with long, muscular legs and the same, non-curved, relatively flat feet that enabled it to walk upright. From the waist up, though, it was more like a chimpanzee: its shoulders are set much lower than ours, and its hands, while still able to manipulate fine objects, were both curved like a chimpanzee's and enormously strong. Commentators have pointed out that these physical features would have helped it climb trees and swing through the branches. It might also have helped this ancient species navigate narrow, precipitous cave systems like the Rising Star.

It's what *H. naledi* may have been doing in the caves that is really exciting. At the bottom of a vertical chute that in some places narrows to less than 20cm (7.9in) in width, and thus extremely difficult to access, explorers found a cache of fossilised *H. naledi* bones. In Professor Berger's opinion, the remains had been placed there on purpose, and had not just arrived there by accident. In other words, and if he's right, *H. naledi* were deliberately burying their dead. This is a ritual activity, and is generally assumed to indicate a high level of intelligence, as well as a sophisticated culture.

As if the discovery of a new and previously unsuspected species wasn't enough to set the world of palaeoanthropology by its ears, some of the physical features of *H. naledi*, and its apparent use of ritual, are still sending out scientific shockwaves.

In September 2017, following the release of his book on the subject of *H. naledi*, Professor Berger said: 'This species of non-human hominin was deliberately disposing of its dead. Taking a dangerous journey into this deep chamber to place its dead or drop its dead into a place that was inaccessible. This is something that prior to this we thought was unique to humans, and perhaps identified [solely] to us, but now don't.'

Other experts expressed doubt about the evidence of ritual behaviour. One suggested that the bones may have ended up at the bottom of the chute following a flood, or been carried there by an ancient watercourse. If so, it still begs the question: why are there absolutely no traces of any *animal* bones having been swept into the pit with *H. naledi*? Wouldn't the fossilised remains of a rat, or a snake, or some other creature unable to escape the flow also have been dumped in the pit? Another expert suggests there may have been a collapse of some kind, which somehow trapped the people whose remains have caused so much excitement. Again though, it seems odd that they should all have been deposited in this tiny, not much more than one-metre square space with no trace of any other flora or fauna whatsoever.

A more plausible explanation is that, while they spent most of their time as hunter-gatherers on the African savannahs, *H. naledi* accessed caves like Dinaledi as places of refuge when they came under threat. In this scenario, a group of people taking refuge from a predator – which may have been animal, or another human-like species – got lost, or became stuck at the bottom of the chute. The fact that they were able to enter the caves in the first place, though, strongly suggests that, like Neanderthals, *H. naledi* had learned to control fire. Without some form of lighting, even with eyes as big and efficient as Gollum's, they could not have moved through these extremely challenging spaces.

A second set of 130 fossils, including a relatively complete adult male skeleton, was discovered in the Lesedi Chamber about 100 metres away from the Dinaledi find. Both chambers are deep within the cave system, which shows no signs of on entrance other than the one so far discovered, and would therefore have been equally dark.

The remains of the Lesedi male, dubbed 'Neo', have been dated to roughly the same period as the remains found in the Dinaledi Chamber, and are causing no less of a stir. Were these bones, too, simply swept into this separate space by the action of water? Or did Neo also get stuck?

Commenting on Africa's largest-ever such find, as well as one of the most important ever made, Professor Chris Stringer of the UK's Natural History Museum, said:

> The fossils display a unique mix of modern and archaic traits and are shaking up our understanding of the origins and diversity of our human lineage. *Homo naledi* highlights, once again, that we can't think of human evolution in terms of ape-like ancestors gradually evolving more modern features in a linear fashion. Instead, multiple human species evolved in parallel and

coexisted, sometimes side-by-side.

Many mysteries surround *Homo naledi*, including how the remains got into the caves, what its tools were like, and how it survived alongside bigger-brained species.

There were never any lakes in these deep and remote caves, so even though their small, slender bodies may have been very similar, the comparison with Gollum, who lived on a subterranean island and caught fish from a boat, is fanciful. But if *H. naledi* weren't hunting for goblins, then what were they doing in there?

Area 51

For decades, sci-fi fans, military buffs and the simply curious have wondered what is going on inside 'Area 51'. A remote and Top Secret US Air Force base located 83 miles (134km) north-north-west of Las Vegas, it has inspired all kinds of rumours and speculation, and any number of books and films. Most of these play a riff on the same theme: that Area 51 is the site of a giant government conspiracy to cover up evidence of official contact with alien life. Many strange and often conflicting eyewitness reports, some of them official US government documents, have been cited to support this claim.

First, let's take a look at what we do know. The Central Intelligence Agency (CIA) created the original, much smaller 6 by 10 miles (9.7 by 16.1km) Area 51 installation in 1955 at the height of the Cold War. Its remote location and ferocious security were meant to keep foreign – and especially Soviet Bloc – intelligence agents from learning anything whatsoever about 'Project Aquatone', the development and testing of the 'U-2' ultra-high-altitude spy plane.

Other super-Top Secret aircraft like the F117A Stealth Fighter were subsequently tested at the site. Unsurprisingly, since it is still in use for secret purposes, the current base remains one of the world's most restricted and forbidden installations. Signs warn in round terms that the armed guards are liable to shoot intruders first, and ask questions later.

Part of Edwards Air Force Base, the facility is nowadays known officially as 'Homey Airport' or Groom Lake. A CIA document created during the Vietnam War nevertheless refers to it as 'Area 51', and this is how most of us have come to know it. The complex is also known as 'Dreamland', 'Paradise Ranch' (to encourage workers to move there) or more commonly, 'The Ranch'. A dedicated, clandestine military airline ships workers in and out of a restricted area of Las Vegas airport.

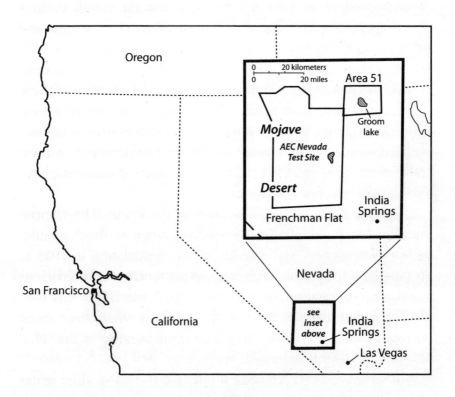

A roughly six by five kilometre (3.7 by 3 mile) area of salt flat at the centre of Area 51, Groom Lake forms part of the Nellis Bombing Range Test Site. Equally barren and featureless, the rest of Area 51 includes runways, barracks, administration blocks, bomb-resistant bunkers and a curious, flat-topped pyramid whose purpose is unknown unless you happen to work there. The base sprawls out across the so-called 'Groom Box', a roughly rectangular slice of desert measuring 23 by 25 miles (37 by 40km). Nothing moves in these enormous and otherwise empty expanses of sagebrush and cactus unless the CIA, the USAF and, quite possibly, the Russians, know about it. Even the rock lizards need to be on their toes.

The fact that, until recently, the US government refused even to acknowledge the existence of Area 51 served only to fuel the 'alien' conspiracy theories. Repeated reports of strange lights and sounds in the sky above the base, as well as the so-called 'sky quakes', did nothing to lessen interest. These involved deafening explosive bangs that shattered the local atmosphere, causing unprepared animals and humans alike to jump sideways out of their skin. There have also been accounts of unexplained fireballs in the skies over the base, and of aircraft travelling at hypersonic speeds trailing circular contrails dubbed 'doughnuts-on-a-rope'.

In August 2013, following decades of secrecy and denial, we found out why: the CIA released documents officially confirming the existence of Area 51, and admitting it had served as a proving ground for one Top Secret aircraft after another. These include the A-12, the YF-12A, the SR-71 Blackbird and the F117-A Stealth Fighter.

Area 51 also plays host to a 'Foreign Materiel Evaluation' programme in which the elite and covert 'Red Hats' squadron flies Russian and other foreign aircraft to evaluate their strengths and weaknesses, and help US 'Top Gun' pilots at the controls of regular USAF fighters learn how to defeat them in aerial combat. What they usually found was that while the aircraft were generally equal in terms of capability, the pilots flying them were not. This led the US military to create specialist advanced tactical training schools to bring pilots up to the required standard. To prevent anyone from watching the dogfights, the airspace over the exercise area was closed. The forbidden box is known as 'Red Square'.

The CIA did not, though, mention any contact with alien intelligence. Nor did it attempt to address accusations that officials at Area 51 were systematically covering up the existence of alien bodies recovered from crashed 'flying saucers' found in the United States. It also kept silent on the notion that government scientists were attempting to build interstellar space craft modelled on the wrecks of alien ships, or trying to reverse engineer the alien technology found on them to produce 'space weapons'.

It was the 'Roswell Incident', as it became known, that gave an early kiss of life to the alien conspiracy theories emanating from US government bases in neighbouring New Mexico. In the last six months of 1947, at the height of what in retrospect seems like a self-intensifying frenzy, there were more than 300 reported Unidentified Flying Object (UFO) sightings in the United States alone, and many more worldwide. In June of that same year – or, according to the Roswell Army Air Field's press release, early July – an unknown flying object crashed to earth on land belonging to the Foster Ranch a few miles north of Roswell, New Mexico. On 14 June, a blocky, no-nonsense ranch foreman named W.W. 'Mack' Brazel was out doing his rounds with his eight-year-old son, Vernon, when he saw what he took to be the debris of a crashed aircraft scattered across the ground. He picked up some of the debris and took it back to the ranch. The 9 July edition of the *Roswell Daily Record* newspaper reported that Brazel initially believed he had found parts of a weather balloon.

Three days later, Brazel showed some of the debris to Chaves

County Sheriff George Wilcox. Wilcox in turn contacted USAF Colonel 'Butch' Blanchard at nearby Roswell Army Air Field (nowadays known as Walker US Air Force Base, and still home to the 509th Bomb Group that dropped the nuclear weapons on Hiroshima and Nagasaki in 1945).

Blanchard in turn informed his superior and Eighth Air Force commanding officer, General Roger W. Ramey. As the buck finally stopped, Ramey ordered the 509th's Intelligence Officer, Major Jesse A. Marcel, to inspect the crash site thoroughly and recover any further items of wreckage he could find. Marcel, who went to view the site in company with another man in plain clothes (perhaps a second intelligence officer named Sheridan Cavill), must have given General Ramey a pretty exciting account of what he had discovered, because later that same day, Ramey, who as yet hadn't even set eyes on the wreckage, gave the order that launched a thousand conspiracy theories. He told Lt. Walter G. Haut, Roswell AAF's Public Information Officer, to issue a press release stating that the base had taken possession of the wreckage of a 'flying disc'.

We're talking about a senior US Air Force officer confirming the existence of what would become much more popularly known as a 'flying saucer'. If that happened today, it would unleash a global media sensation. Twitter storms would roll and thunder across the Internet. Rolling news would broadcast updates around the clock. As it was, when the news hit the airwaves on 8 July 1947 the networks did start buzzing, but compared to current media broadsides, its reach and effect were relatively limited.

General Ramey ordered the wreckage to be shipped to him at Fort Worth, Texas, where he and the base Weather Officer, among others, examined it. That same day, Ramey ordered the release of a new press statement, claiming that what Mr Brazel had actually discovered was not, after all, the remains of a 'flying disc', but as the ranch foreman had himself supposed, pieces of a crashed weather balloon. The new claim appeared on 9 July 1947:

> The balloon which held it up, if that was how it worked, must have been 12 feet long, (Brazel) felt, measuring the distance by the size of the room in which he sat. The rubber was smoky gray in color and scattered over an area about 200 yards in diameter. When the debris was gathered up, the tinfoil, paper, tape, and sticks made a bundle about three feet long and 7 or 8 inches thick, while the rubber made a bundle about 18 or 20 inches long and about 8 inches thick. In all, he estimated, the entire lot would have weighed maybe five pounds. There was no sign of any metal in the area which might have been used for an engine, and no sign of any propellers of any kind, although at least one paper fin had been glued onto some of the tinfoil. There were no words to be found anywhere on the instrument, although there were letters on some of the parts. Considerable Scotch tape and some tape with flowers printed upon it had been used in the construction. No strings or wires were to be found but there were some eyelets in the paper to indicate that some sort of attachment may have been used.

The Army issued a series of photographs taken in his office of the general and another serviceman examining a collection of what to the uneducated but sceptical eye look very much like non-alien remains.

On the same day, the *Roswell Daily Record* ran a new story with the headline: 'Harassed Rancher Who Located "Saucer" Sorry He Told About It.' In the article, Mack Brazel was quoted as saying that all he'd actually found out in the desert that day was, 'rubber strips, tinfoil, a rather tough paper and sticks'. The fact that the man who'd actually found the crash debris seemed to be confirming Ramey's new version of events more or less killed the entire story, so that it all but disappeared off the media radar for another 31 years.

Then, in 1978, nuclear physicist and UFO researcher Stanton Friedman interviewed the now retired Major Jesse Marcel. In a complete contradiction of his earlier statements, Marcel categorically denied that the wreckage he'd been ordered to recover at Roswell had ever, in his considered opinion, been anything to do with a weather balloon. Commenting on some of the metal he'd found, he said:

> it felt like you had nothing in your hands; it wasn't any thicker than the foil out of a pack of cigarettes. But the thing about it that got me is that you couldn't even bend it, you couldn't dent it, even a sledgehammer would bounce off of it.
>
> I knew that I had never seen anything like that before . . . It was not anything from this Earth, that I'm quite sure of . . . Being an intelligence officer I was familiar with just about all materials used in aircraft and/or air travel. This was nothing like that. It could not have been.

Marcel further claimed that on arrival at Fort Worth, he'd spread out the Roswell crash debris on Ramey's desk. The general then asked him to go through with him into the map room, so that Marcel could pinpoint the exact location of the crash. By the time they returned to the general's office, Marcel claims something very strange had happened: the pieces of wreckage he'd left on the desk had disappeared – and in their place were the more-or-less damaged remains of a high-altitude weather balloon. Marcel says he stood there scratching his head as the press photographers streamed in past him.

Friedman interviewed a succession of witnesses, including Mack Brazel, who also now went back on his earlier story.

Having also spoken with Sheriff Wilcox, Colonel Blanchard and Walter Haut, Friedman concluded that the Roswell Incident was a 'Cosmic Watergate' – an official cover-up that was hiding evidence of the crashed spacecraft and its saucer-eyed occupants. One of the most secure and closely guarded military installations in the whole of the United States, Area 51 fell under immediate suspicion as the place where this red-hot evidence of alien life was being concealed.

As if all of this wasn't enough to stir the conspiracy pot, in 1989 a Ballard, New Mexico mortuary worker named Glenn Dennis contacted a telephone hotline that had been set up to take calls from people with information about alien activity. Dennis told the operator that at the time of the 'Roswell crash' in 1947, he had been in charge of the Ballard Funeral Home's military contract. This included the supply of mortuary and ambulance services for the nearby Roswell Army Air Field.

Dennis claimed that in July of that same year, Roswell's base mortuary officer had asked him whether the Ballard funeral home could provide five child-sized, hermetically sealed coffins. In a second phone call, the same officer supposedly asked Dennis if he could advise him on mortuary procedures 'for bodies that have been lying in the desert for a long time'.

Shortly after these odd, alleged calls, Dennis says he picked up an injured US serviceman and drove him to Roswell in an ambulance. Inside the base, he said he saw strange wreckage with unknown writing on it. At this point, Dennis claims a 'nervous' female Army nurse approached him and told him he had to leave the facility. Next day, though, Dennis says the same unnamed nurse contacted him again, this time covertly, and asked him to meet her at the base Officers' Club. When he arrived and they were alone, Dennis claims she gave him details of three 'alien autopsies' that she said had taken place inside the base mortuary, and at which she also told him she had personally assisted. To back up her story, 'Nurse X', as she became known, made some drawings of the 'alien' corpses, which Dennis, together with all the other information he'd amassed, kept secret until disclosing them in the course of the dramatic 1989 phone-in.

By now enjoying some fame and celebrity, in 1991 and to back up his claims of having sighted alien remains inside Roswell AAFB, Dennis released the following affidavit:

AFFIDAVIT OF GLENN DENNIS

(1) My name is Glenn Dennis

(2) My address is: XXXXXXXXXX

(3) I am ( ) employed as: _____
_____ ( ) retired,

(4) In July 1947, I was a mortician, working for
the Ballard Funeral Home in Roswell, which had
a contract to provide mortuary services for the
Roswell Army Air Field. One afternoon, around 1:15
or 1:30, I received a call from the base mortuary officer who asked what was the smallest size
hermetically sealed casket that we had in stock.
He said, "We need to know this in case something
comes up in the future." He asked how long it
would take to get one, and I assured him I could
get one for him the following day. He said he
would call back if they needed one.

(5) About 45 minutes to an hour later, he called back and asked me to describe the preparation for bodies that had been lying out on the desert for a period of time. Before I could answer, he said he specifically wanted to know what effect the preparation procedures would have on the body's chemical compounds, blood and tissues. I explained that our chemicals were mainly strong solutions of formaldehyde and water, and that the procedure would probably alter the body's chemical composition. I offered to come out to the base to assist with any problem he might have, but he reiterated that the information was for future use. I suggested that if he had such a situation that I would try to freeze the body in dry ice for storage and transportation.

(6) Approximately an hour or an hour and 15 minutes later, I got a call to transport a serviceman who had a laceration on his head and perhaps a fractured nose. I gave him first aid and drove him out to the base. I got there around 5:00 PM.

(7) Although I was a civilian, I usually had free access on the base because they knew me. I drove the ambulance around to the back of the base infirmary and parked it next to another ambulance. The door was open and inside I saw some wreckage. There were several pieces which looked like the bottom of a canoe, about three feet in length. It resembled stainless steel with a purple hue, as if it had been exposed to high temperature. There was some strange-looking writing on the material

resembling Egyptian hieroglyphics. Also there were two MPs present.

(8) I checked the airman in and went to the staff lounge to have a Coke. I intended to look for a nurse, a 2nd Lieutenant, who had been commissioned about three months earlier right out of college. She was 23 years of age at the time (I was 22). I saw her coming out of one of the examining rooms with a cloth over her mouth. She said, "My gosh, get out of here or you're going to be in a lot of trouble." She went into another door where a Captain stood. He asked me who I was and what I was doing here. I told him, and he instructed me to stay there. I said, "It looks like you've got a crash; would you like me to get ready?" He told me to stay right there. Then two MPs came up and began to escort me out of the infirmary. They said they had orders to follow me out to the funeral home.

(9) We got about 10 or 15 feet when I heard a voice say, "We're not through with that SOB. Bring him back." There was another Captain, a redhead with the meanest-looking eyes I had ever seen, who said, "You did not see anything, there was no crash here, and if you say anything you could get into a lot of trouble." I said, "Hey look mister, I'm a civilian and you can't do a damn thing to me." He said, "Yes we can; somebody will be picking your bones out of the sand." There was a black Sergeant with a pad in his hand who said, "He would make good dog food for our dogs." The

Captain said, "Get the SOB out." The MPs followed me back to the funeral home.

(10) The next day, I tried to call the nurse to see what was going on. About 11:00 AM, she called the funeral home and said, "I need to talk to you." We agreed to meet at the officers club. She was very upset. She said, "Before I talk to you, you have to give me a sacred oath that you will never mention my name, because I could get into a lot of trouble." I agreed.

(11) She said she had gone to get supplies in a room where two doctors were performing a preliminary autopsy. The doctors said they needed her to take notes during the procedure. She said she had never smelled anything so horrible in her life, and the sight was the most gruesome she had ever seen. She said, "This was something no one has ever seen." As she spoke, I was concerned that she might go into shock.

(12) She drew me a diagram of the bodies, including an arm with a hand that had only four fingers; the doctors noted that on the end of the fingers were little pads resembling suction cups. She said the head was disproportionately large for the body; the eyes were deeply set; the skulls were flexible; the nose was concave with only two orifices;the mouth was a fine slit, and the doctors said there was heavy cartilage instead of teeth. The ears were only small orifices with flaps. They had no hair, and the skin was black – perhaps due

to exposure in the sun. She gave me the drawings.

(13) There were three bodies; two were very
mangled and dismembered, as if destroyed by
predators; one was fairly intact. They were three-
and-a-half to four feet tall. She told me the
doctors said, "This isn't anything we've ever seen
before; there's nothing in the medical textbooks
like this." She said she and the doctors became
ill. They had to turn off the air conditioning and
were afraid the smell would go through the hospital. They had to move the operation to an airplane
hangar.

(14) I drove her back to the officers' barracks.
The next day I called the hospital to see how she
was, and they said she wasn't available. I tried
to get her for several days, and finally got one of
the nurses who said the Lieutenant had been transferred out with some other personnel. About 10
days to two weeks later, I got a letter from her
with an APO number. She indicated we could discuss
the incident by letter in the future. I wrote back
to her and about two weeks later the letter came
back marked "Return to Sender - DECEASED." Later,
one of the nurses at the base said the rumor was
that she and five other nurses had been on a training mission and had been killed in a plane crash.

(15) Sheriff George Wilcox and my father were very
close friends. The Sheriff went to my folks' house
the morning after the events at the base and said
to my father, "I don't know what kind of trouble

Glenn's in, but you tell your son that he doesn't know anything and hasn't seen anything at the base." He added, "They want you and your wife's name, and they want your and your children's addresses.' My father immediately drove to the funeral home and asked me what kind of trouble I was in. He related the conversation with Sheriff Wilcox, and so I told him about the events of the previous day. He is the only person to whom I have told this story until recently.

(16) I had filed away the sketches the nurse gave me that day. Recently, at the request of a researcher, I tried to locate my personal files at the funeral home, but they had all been destroyed.

(17) I have not been paid or given anything of value to make this statement, which is the truth to the best of my recollection.

Signed: Glenn Dennis
Date: 8-7-91

Signature witnessed by:
Walter G. Haut

Anti-conspiracy researchers immediately got busy, trashing all of Dennis's claims as spurious. To prove that they were bogus, the sceptics focused their investigations on the identity of 'Nurse X'. Asked to provide this, Dennis said that she had been 'transferred to England' immediately after their meeting in the Officers' Club. Dennis further claimed that when he subsequently wrote to her precisely in order to get further testimony from her about the 'alien bodies', the letter came back marked 'Deceased', and he was told that she had died in a military air crash.

No records, however, have ever been found of a US military – or, for that matter, any other – air crash at or around the time in question. Later, in an interview published in the April 1992 edition of the *MUFON UFO Journal*, Dennis changed his story, telling journalists: 'I never did try and contact her . . . She did join an order [became a nun] after she got out of the Army.' Given that in many religious orders, nuns are confined to their convents, have little contact with the outside world and are required to remain silent, this explanation struck the unbelievers as a little convenient.

Under further pressure to prove he was telling the truth, Dennis finally agreed to release the identity of the ever-elusive Nurse X. She was, he now disclosed, named Naomi Maria Self. An excellent article posted on the online roswellfiles.com website notes: 'The "Morning Reports" that list all military personnel still exists for the Roswell Army Air Field (RAAF) for July 1947. They show that there were only five nurses assigned to RAAF during July 1947, and none of these were suddenly transferred to England or anywhere overseas. None of the nurses was named Naomi Maria Self, or had any name resembling that name. Thorough searches of the files in the National Personnel Records Center failed to find anyone by that name that had ever served in the military.'

Challenged on that score, Dennis changed his story once again, saying that: 'I gave you a phony name, because I promised her [Nurse X] that I would never reveal it to anyone.'

It didn't stop there. Despite the lack of hard written evidence, or the actual appearance of Nurse X, several other people came forward to corroborate at least some elements of Dennis's account. They include a former Roswell Army Air Force base military policeman named L.M. Hall, who signed the following affidavit in 1993:

AFFIDAVIT OF L.M. HALL

(1) My name is L. M. Hall

(2) My address is: XXXXXXXXXX

(3) I am ( ) employed as: _____
    _____ (x) retired,

(4) I came to Roswell, New Mexico, in 1943, while serving in the Army Air Force. I was a military policeman and investigator at Roswell Army Air Field (RAAF). In 1946, after being discharged from the service, I joined the Roswell Police Department, and in 1964 I was appointed chief of police, serving for 14 and a half years. I am now a member of the Roswell City Council.

(5) In 1947, I was a motorcycle officer, with patrol duty on South Main Street, between town and RAAF. I and other police officers would often take our breaks in the small lounge at the Ballard Funeral Home at 910 South Main, where Glenn Dennis worked. I had gotten to know Glenn when I was a base MP because he made ambulance calls to the base under a contract Ballard's had, so I would sometimes have coffee with him if he was at work when I stopped in.

(6) One day in July 1947, I was at Ballard's on a break, and Glenn and I were in the driveway "batting the breeze." I was sitting on my motorcycle, and Glenn stood nearby. He remarked, "I had a funny call from the base. They wanted to know if we had several baby caskets." Then he started laughing and said, "I asked what for, and they said they wanted to bury [or ship] those aliens," something to that effect. I thought it was one of those "gotcha" jokes, so I didn't bite. He never said anything else about it, and I didn't either.

(7) I believe our conversation took place couple of days after the stories about a crashed flying saucer appeared in the Roswell papers.

(8) I have not been paid or given anything of value to make this statement, which is the truth to the best of my recollection.

Signed: L. M. Hall
Date: 9-15-93

Signature witnessed by:
No one present to witness

In the same year that Dennis broke his story, 1989, a man claiming to be a Massachusetts Institute of Technology (MIT)-qualified physicist dragged Area 51 into public view for the first time. Speaking under the pseudonym 'Dennis' and with his features blacked-out, Bob Lazar told a reporter on local Las Vegas television station KLAS that 'S-4', a super-secret scientific facility he said existed inside Area 51, had employed him in its early years to 'reverse engineer' alien technology. He claimed that when he arrived at S-4, he saw not one, but no fewer than nine extraterrestrial spacecraft. Some were in pristine condition, others a little the worse for wear. This was exactly what many in the UFO community had always suspected. Lazar also said that the extraterrestrial spacecraft he'd studied at S-4 included the 'flying disc' that had supposedly crashed at Roswell.

Again, the problem for the sceptics was the lack of any hard evidence. For one thing, there was no record of a Robert Lazar ever having studied at MIT. Challenged but not fazed, Lazar said that the US government had made sure his name was 'scrubbed' from the Institute's records as part of a conspiracy to conceal the evidence of alien contact from the public. But another problem with Lazar's History is his 1959 birth date, which makes his claims of working at Area 51 'in the early years of its existence' problematic.

Whatever their truth, none of these claims and counter-claims did the ever-growing worldwide interest in UFOs, Area 51, Roswell or the business opportunities that came with these juicy stories, any harm at all. To keep the flood of UFO tourism flowing, the Nevada state administration even named State Highway 375, which skirts Area 51, 'The Extraterrestrial Highway'.

Has there ever been any clear and uncontested evidence that alien life forms and extraterrestrial spacecraft crashed near Roswell, and were examined at Area 51? Depends on your point of view. In 1995, a man named Ray Santill released grainy black-and-white video footage that supposedly showed a dead alien recovered from the Roswell crash site undergoing autopsy. The footage, which achieved global fame, caused a great deal of controversy – which persisted even after Santill himself admitted to reporter Eamonn Holmes in the April 2006 Sky

TV documentary *Eamonn Investigates: Alien Autopsy* that his film was a 'reconstruction', that incorporated only a few frames of the original – and supposedly genuine – footage.

Santill and fellow-producer Gary Shoefield told Holmes that they had 'restored' the original footage with the help of artist and sculptor John Humphreys, in a flat in Camden Town, London. They said that Humphreys constructed a set and created two 'alien bodies' using plaster casts, chicken entrails, sheep brains artistically arranged in raspberry jam, and bone joints obtained from the famous Smithfield meat market. Throughout the documentary, Holmes refers to Santill's film as 'a fake'. Santill told Holmes that he had exercised artistic licence when it came to the alien symbols and artefacts, such as the six-finger control panels, that appear in the 'reconstructed' film.

In September 1994, following years of relentless public and media pressure, the USAF released an official report on the Roswell Incident. It admitted that the 'weather balloon' story originally issued to explain the wreckage found on the Foster Ranch in 1947 had been a cover-up – but not of any alien activity. Instead, the debris was from a high-altitude balloon released as part of a Top Secret programme codenamed 'Project Mogul'. The cover-up had only been put in place to conceal this.

This new claim also bears examination. There was, definitely, a Top Secret programme of that name. Conducted between 1947 and 1949, Project Mogul saw scientists and engineers attach super-sensitive microphones to high-altitude balloons, often connected one to another in a kind of airborne daisy-chain, to see if they could detect underground Soviet nuclear bomb tests, and to assess the size of the explosions. Naturally, this second revision of events at Roswell – and the admission that the weather balloon story had been officially fabricated – added even more fuel to the conspiracy fire.

The debate might once again have died away, had it not been

for another unexpected piece of official news. In December 2017, the *New York Times* reported that between the years 2007 and 2012, the Department of Defense had spent $22m on what it termed the 'Advanced Aerospace Threat Identification Program'.

Finally, under further pressure, the Pentagon confirmed that there had, after all, been a government programme to collect and analyse what it called 'anomalous aerospace threats' – or UFOs piloted by hostile aliens to the rest of us. Run by military intelligence official Luis Elizondo from an office on the fifth floor of the Pentagon's C Ring, in simple terms the Advanced Aerospace Threat Identification Program investigated sightings of UFOs. Here was the kicker: it was US military pilots themselves who had reported most of the mysterious sightings. This was great stuff. US military pilots are not selected on the grounds of their over-active imaginations, or hysterical tendencies. So what was going on?

As part of the newfound US government openness, the Department of Defense released a number of strange, and, it has to be said, slightly chilling videos. Most striking among these was a clip of a UFO being tracked by US Navy pilots off the coast of San Diego in 2004.* While disturbing to the untrained – and perhaps even, the trained – eye, the DoD videos are very unclear. They don't, of themselves, add up to incontrovertible evidence of alien visitations, but combined with the admission that there had, after all, been a concerted government programme to identify and if necessary counter alien threats, they do leave us wondering – is there something behind what many have dismissed as the UFO conspiracy business after all?

Over the past 60 years, no fewer than 2,000 military and

* See: https://www.nytimes.com/2017/12/16/us/politics/pentagon-program-ufo-harry-reid.html

civilian aircraft are said to have crashed or disappeared over the hostile landscape that surrounds Area 51. Speculation that these losses, too, were connected to covert Top Secret activity at the base involving aliens received a dent when it was shown that, in many cases, aircraft were falling prey to sudden, high-speed and often deadly wind-shear anomalies caused by a combination of weather and the special topographical conditions of the Sierra Nevada mountains. And yet, at more than 30 losses a year, that is one hell of a lot of crashed and missing aircraft.

The wheels of government turn slowly, but the Internet knows few bounds. In 2003, satellite photographs of Area 51 published on the net finally forced the US government to acknowledge its existence. Asked what went on at the base, Assistant Secretary of Defense Kenneth H. Baconfelt struck a laconic note: 'Very little . . . we have a right, as a sovereign nation – in fact, a responsibility to the citizens of the United States – to develop various weapons from time to time. Sometimes, these weapons are developed in classified locations . . . I think I can say beyond a shadow of doubt that we have no classified program that relies on aliens from outer space.'

Why is it hard to believe that this is the last word we shall ever hear on the mystery of Area 51?

The Zodiac Killer

'This is the Zodiac speaking.'

A homicidal maniac uttered these chilling words. Beginning in the late 1960s, the self-styled 'Zodiac' killer carried out a brutal killing spree that terrorised the people of central north-western California.

Although he unleashed two of his verified attacks in broad daylight, the Zodiac killer has never been caught, and may still be at large. For nearly five decades since his last known murder of a San Francisco taxi driver in October 1969, the case has stymied law enforcement officials, professional and amateur code breakers and criminologists alike. The FBI, the California Department of Justice, the San Francisco Police Department (SFPD) and several local California jurisdictions maintain open case files on the homicides, as yet to no avail. How has this killer managed to elude so many law enforcement agencies for so long?

The Zodiac's cruel murders and taunting, cryptic puzzles have inspired no fewer than 12 films and documentaries, and he pops up as a virtual character in at least seven popular video games. Still, to this day, there are hundreds of books, blogs, and all kinds of Internet sites devoted to solving the cryptic clues he left to his identity.

Officially, investigators confirm the Zodiac targeted seven victims, two of whom survived. In letters to the media, however, the Zodiac himself claimed to have murdered 37 people. If true, this would make him one of the most prolific serial killers in history.

In 1969, Vallejo was a sleepy, middle class waterfront town in the San Pablo Bay area north of San Francisco. A major local crime at that time would have been a burglary or a stolen car. Yet it was here, on the evening of 20 December 1968, that the Zodiac assaulted his first two known victims: 17-year-old David Faraday and 16-year-old Betty Lou Jensen.

The pair had originally been going to attend a school Christmas concert, close to Betty Lou's home on Ridgewood Court. Instead, as teenagers often do, they changed their plans at the last minute, grabbing a bite to eat at a local restaurant and then driving out to a remote countryside spot to the east of Vallejo. Although it was a cold December night, red-haired, snub-nosed Betty Lou was wearing her best dress: lilac, with a white lace collar. It was the first time she had ever been allowed out on a date.

At around 10:15 p.m., Faraday pulled off Lake Herman Road and parked his mother's prized two-tone Rambler sedan on an isolated, unlit gravel pull-off area just outside the city limits that formed part of the entrance to Benicia Water pumping station. Betty Lou took off her white fake fur coat and laid it on the rear seat.

Just before 11:00 p.m., a set of headlights blazed from the darkness. Seconds later, a car pulled up under the bright yellow traffic sign at the edge of the road. The driver approached the Rambler and ordered the couple to get out. As a startled Faraday began opening the door, the unknown killer shot him at point blank range, blasting straight through the window. The bullet tore through the young man's left ear and travelled on into his head. Betty Lou jumped out of the car and started running. She made no more than four paces. The gunman shot her five times in the back and then drove away.

A few minutes later, a local woman named Stella Borges found the couple and called the emergency services. When the police arrived, they found Betty Lou lying dead on the ground a few yards away from the Rambler. David Faraday was still alive. He was clasping his gold class ring tight between his thumb and index finger, as if he'd been trying to stop someone wrenching it free. He died on the way to hospital without being able to describe his attacker.

Ten cartridge cases were recovered at the Lake Herman crime scene, but only nine were forensically examined. The ammunition was identified as .22 calibre Winchester Western Super X, copper-coated, long rifle, possibly fired from a J. C. Higgins Model 80 semi-automatic pistol. The Solano County Sheriff's Department investigated the double-murder, but concluded the attack had been carried out at random. Despite the evidence of tyre and boot tracks and the spent bullet casings, investigating officers were unable to find any links or leads to the killer. No one was ever arrested for the crime.

The Zodiac killer struck again a little over six months later. Once again, his target was a young courting couple – and the similarities between the two cases were striking.

Married and with a young child, Darlene Ferrin lived at 1300 Virginia Street, Vallejo, and worked as a waitress at Terry's Waffle Shop on Magazine Street. On the evening of 4 July 1969, Darlene was with her sister, Christina Suennan, and her husband, Dean Ferrin, at the place where he worked on Tennessee Street. At about 10:30 p.m., Darlene announced that she was going to drive Christina home, and then go on home herself. When she did arrive back at approximately 11:30 p.m., she told her two schoolgirl babysitters that her husband's boss, Bill Lee, had asked her to buy some fireworks so that everyone could have an impromptu Independence Day party. She left the house about ten minutes later wearing a black dress with a broad 'V' neck and blue shoes.

Instead of going to buy fireworks, Darlene Ferrin headed for 864 Beechwood Avenue, the home of 19-year-old Michael Renault Mageau. She arrived there at approximately 11:45 p.m. A slightly odd feature of this second case is that Dean Ferrin apparently turned a blind eye to his wife's love affairs with other men.

Snub-nosed, dark and good-looking, Mageau, who was very thin and quick in his movements, scrambled into Darlene's light-brown 1963 Chevrolet Corvair. The couple drove towards Mr. Ed's Diner on Springs Road. Then, changing plans on the hop and in an echo of the previous attack, they pulled a 180-degree turn and headed for Blue Rock Springs Park, a local beauty spot. The area was at the time still relatively undeveloped. The park was quiet, very poorly lit at night, and so perfect for clandestine lovers. The couple turned into the 'lovers' lane' area at about five minutes to midnight and rumbled to a stop. Despite the lateness of the hour, the night was still sultry. Whether or not Ferrin and Mageau knew it, they were less than four miles from the spot where, just before Christmas the previous year, Betty Lou and David had been fatally shot. Darlene put some music on the car radio and turned the lights off. The precise time line from this moment on is unclear, but events now unfolded very quickly.

Shortly afterwards, cars with what Mageau called 'young kids' in them pulled into the same parking lot. The teenagers horsed around for a minute or two, let off a few firecrackers, then jumped back into their vehicles and sped away. It was now almost exactly midnight.

A new car now turned into the parking lot and pulled up,

close to the left side of Darlene's car. The driver switched off his lights and sat there for a minute. Mageau later claimed he asked Darlene if she knew the identity of the stranger sitting motionless at the wheel of the other vehicle. He says she told him, 'He's just jealous,' thereby suggesting she knew the watching driver well. The newcomer started up his car again and disappeared.

Three or four minutes later, what was probably the same car rolled back into the lot. This time, the driver pulled up ten feet behind and slightly to the right of Darlene's Corvair. Leaving his headlights on full beam, he got out and began walking towards the couple. A stark silhouette against the glare, the man cut a menacing figure.

Growing nervous, Mageau noticed the stranger was holding 'a high-power flashlight, the kind you carry with a handle'. But the man was walking casually and confidently towards them, as if he had every right to be there. Assuming from his bearing and the torch that he was a law enforcement officer, Mageau rolled down his window and reached for his ID. Without a word, the stranger raised a 9mm Luger pistol, pointed it into Mageau's face and opened fire.

The first bullet struck the nineteen-year-old just beneath and a little forward of the right ear, went through his tongue, exited through his left cheek and then hit Darlene in the left side. More bullets hit Mageau in the left shoulder, elbow and ribs, and a fifth hit him in the knee. The combined force of these and his own survival instinct propelled him backwards and into the rear seat. Police believe he raised his legs and curled up, thrashed around for a moment and then fell back. Darlene was slumped motionless behind the wheel, covered in blood. As she fell she knocked a control stalk, so that the Corvair's left-hand indicator began blinking on and off.

Assuming his victims were dead, the assailant turned and walked back towards his own vehicle. Mageau then gave a cry. The killer stopped, returned and fired two more rounds apiece into the victims. At this point Darlene most likely took a second slug into her right-side ribs. Then, and still without having uttered a word, the killer got back in his car and drove off in the direction of Springs Road.

Lying in bed 300 yards away, young George Bryant, the son of the park caretaker, heard what he believed could have been shots, but might also have been firecrackers. It was the Fourth of July, and a bit of high-spirited behaviour was normal, so Bryant did not initially report what he had heard to the police. Interviewed later, he told them he'd heard a car that 'burned rubber' as it roared away at high speed.

Mageau was still alive – but only just. He grappled with the door handle and fell out onto the ground. Three more teenaged holiday revellers now pulled into the parking lot. They spotted Mageau immediately. Horrified by the blood that had leaked from his multiple injuries, they stared at him. He looked back up at them and croaked, 'Help! Help!' The trio jumped back into their vehicle, raced over to Castlewood Drive where one of them, Jerry, lived, and called the police.

At that moment, Detective Sergeants John Lanch and Ed Rust of Vallejo Police Department were in plain clothes on a three-to-midnight shift, patrolling in the old part of town. Shortly after midnight, the radio crackled into life: there was a report of a shooting at Blue Rock Springs Park. Assuming it was likely nothing more than Independence Day firecrackers, Lanch was reluctant to go up there so near to the end of his shift. Rust, at the wheel, decided it was worth investigating, but as the junior partner, all he could do was ease over in the general direction of the park. Then a second, and much more urgent report came through from police dispatch: 'Shots fired at Blue Rock Springs.' Rust put pedal to the metal, and they arrived at the parking lot a few minutes later.

A third Vallejo PD police officer, Richard Hoffman, was already on the scene. Not only was Hoffman the first police responder, he had swung by that very same parking lot about half an hour earlier. In subsequent interviews, Hoffman said he had gone there to 'check for teenagers'. The timings strongly suggest that Hoffman had been at the crime scene immediately before the attack, and should have noticed Darlene Ferrin's Corvair. Yet he reported that he had neither seen nor heard anything, and that there were no vehicles in the lot when he looked it over. When the first reports of gunfire came in, Hoffman said, 'I wasn't far away, so I turned around . . . and told dispatch I was going to go out there to check on that report.'

Hoffman found Michael Mageau lying on his back on the ground next to the Corvair and bent to help him. Mageau tried to reach for Hoffman, and may have tried to speak; but the blood pooling in his throat meant that he could only make a gurgling sound. The passenger door was standing open. Hoffman looked across and saw that the female driver, later identified as Darlene Ferrin, had also been shot. Much of the car's interior gleamed with blood. The Corvair's headlights were now back on, but whether that was because Darlene had tried to use them to attract attention before she lost consciousness was never established. Hoffman chalked around Mageau's body: he also removed some of the victim's belongings, including his wallet.

Rust and Lanch now arrived on the scene. Rust asked Hoffman, 'What have we got here?' Hoffman said, 'I got the driver and this guy here . . . they've both been shot.' Rust walked around the car to the driver's side. He saw a young female covered in blood at the wheel, still breathing and with her eyes very slightly open. Leaning in as close as he could, he asked her, 'What happened?' Darlene mumbled something, but Rust was unable to make out any of the words.

The ambulance arrived. Hoffman got in and sat close to

Darlene, in case she said anything, but 'There was no talking to that girl.' As the ambulance attendant attempted to give her CPR, air whistled out through the bullet wounds in Ferrin's chest.

Back at the crime scene, Rust spotted a cartridge case on the ground where Mageau had been lying. It was from a 9mm Parabellum round. Forensic officers retrieved six more cartridge cases from the right side of the Corvair, and a further two from the rear passenger side footwell. The killer had fired nine shots in all.

The 'Lost' Forty Minutes

At 12:40 a.m. on 5 July, approximately 40 minutes after the assault, 26-year-old Vallejo police dispatcher Nancy Slover took a call. The male voice on the line came as a deep, dead slow monotone: 'I want to report a double murder.' The call was traced to a public phone booth at the Union 76 gas station on Springs Road and Tuolumne – just a few hundred metres from Darlene Ferrin's home. Slover said she got a 'creepy feeling' from the voice at the end of the line. She asked the caller for his name and location, but he ignored her.

Instead, he said, 'If you will go one mile east on Columbus Parkway to a public park, you will find the kids in a brown car. They were shot with a 9mm Luger. I also killed those kids last year . . .' Then, with a final 'Goodbye', he hung up. One of only three people ever to speak with him directly, Slover reported that the Zodiac killer said the word 'Goodbye' in a slow, mocking tone, dragging out the words as if to taunt her. It was both a confession and a warning. Since police recording equipment for incoming telephone calls wasn't in widespread use at the time, there is no recording of the call.

By 'last year' police reasoned the caller must mean the double homicide of David Faraday and Betty Lou Jensen at Lake Herman – not just because of the call, but because the modus operandi (MO) of both crimes was so similar.

There are plenty of elements in the Ferrin–Mageau attack that don't quite add up: first among these is George Bryant's account. It tallies with Mageau's in that he heard 'laughing and a few firecrackers being set off, then what sounded like a series of gunshots'. Yet the description of a car 'taking off at high speed and burning rubber' does not accord with what Mageau or the Zodiac himself eventually told the police. In Mageau's account, the attacker, a well-built white male of between 30 and 40 years old, with a 'strong' face and brown wavy hair, got calmly back into his car and drove quietly away as if nothing had happened.

Did a personal motive play a part in the murder of Darlene Ferrin? Darlene's sister Pamela Huckaby always claimed that a man who resembled the sketches of the Zodiac killer had been stalking 'Dee' for months before her death. Huckaby also said that Darlene had known Betty Lou Jensen – although there is no hard evidence for the link. Intriguingly, though, the initial police report states 'Jealousy/Revenge' as the motive for the shootings.

As if to bear out this version of events, survivor Michael Mageau later claimed in television documentaries that shortly before her murder, Darlene had told him that she thought a former boyfriend, 'Richard', was at the wheel of the vehicle that pulled up next to them in Blue Rock Springs that night. Mageau says she told him Richard would kill her if he found out about the two of them. Mageau, who suffered serious brain trauma and life-changing injuries in the attack, admits he didn't report this conversation to the police at the time. Which leaves us wondering: if the story is true, then who was 'Richard' – and is he the Zodiac killer?

The brutal murders ran a hot wire of shock throughout the whole Vallejo-Benicia area, and beyond. The proximity of the two crimes, the clear local knowledge of where best to predate on courting couples and the calm audacity with which they were committed strongly suggested that the killer was a local who felt secure on his home turf.

The Killer Goes Public

In the wake of this second attack, the Zodiac killer sent three almost identical letters to three California newspapers, all postmarked 31 July 1969. In these he claimed responsibility for both the Lake Herman and Vallejo attacks. He also gave details of the victims, the weapons, the number of shots fired and the (Winchester) 'Super X' brand of ammunition that he said he'd used. In true psychopath style, he taunted: 'The police shall never catch me, because I have been too clever for them.'

The *Vallejo Times-Herald* version of the letter reads as follows:

Dear Editor
I am the killer of the 2 teen-agers last Christmass at Lake Herman and the Girl last 4th of July. To Prove this I shall state some facts which only I + the police know.
Christmass
1 Brand name of ammo Super X
2 10 Shots fired
3 Boy was on back feet to car
4 Girl was lyeing on right side
feet to west
4th of July
1 Girl was wearing patterned Pants

2 Boy was also shot in knee

3 Brand name of ammo was Western

Here is a cyipher or that is part of one. the other 2 parts have been mailed to the S.F. Examiner + the S.F. Chronicle I want you to print this cipher on your frunt page by Fry Afternoon Aug 1-69, If you do not do this I will go on a kill ram page Fry night that will last the whole week end.

I will cruse around and pick of all stray people or coupples that are alone then move on to kill some more untill I have killed over a dozen people

The letter to the *San Francisco Chronicle* was worded slightly differently, beginning, 'This is the killer,' and not, 'I am the killer,' and mentioning a golf course.

In all three versions of the letter, the author threatened that unless the letters and ciphers were published by Friday, 1 August, he would 'go on a kill rampage Friday night. I will cruise around all weekend killing lone people in the night, then move on to kill again, until I end up with a dozen people over the weekend.' The letters were duly published.

Each of these three initial letters contained one-third of an enciphered message. Known as the 'Z Ciphers', and numbered according to how many symbols each message included, these codes – or cryptograms – became the subject of widespread professional and amateur code-breaking attempts that continue to this day.

Known as 'Z 408', the three-part cipher is the longest of all the Zodiac codes. Each of the three encoded messages was made up of 8x17 symbols, making 408 in total. Across the world, people set about attempting to decipher it.

There are a number of curious facts about the style and execution of these letters. They contain some very poor spelling

– 'cyipher', 'coupples', 'Christmass', 'frunt' and so on in the first. Unless deliberate, these mistakes suggest a low level of education, not least in the English language. At the same time, the three-part code forms a fairly complex cipher, which suggests a high level of intelligence, and possibly some background knowledge or training in the field of cryptography. The killer also appears to have been generally clued-up about geographical direction, as in the comment, 'Girl was lyeing on right side feet to west.' Combined with the obvious levels of planning that he put into the crimes, this knowledge invites us to speculate that he had undergone some kind of military training. The other curious thing is the 'crosshairs' signature, which again strikes something of a military note. It also, and more importantly, betrays a wish to self-brand, an overweening ego, and delusions of grandeur.

He might have had haphazard spelling and grammar, but the Zodiac killer's careful MO indicates an organised personality. The fact that he had worked out in advance what to do to his victims and how to do it, while at the same time selecting them at random in places he had also picked out beforehand, demonstrates a high degree of cunning and premeditation. The taunting of both law enforcement agencies and the public at large bears witness to a confident, vindictive and boastful psychopath.

The killer may have had some training in cryptology, but it wasn't enough to prevent Salinas schoolteachers Bettye June and Donald Harden cracking the 408 cipher, and sending their solution to the *San Francisco Chronicle* a few days later. Using classic letter/cryptogram frequency analysis, Bettye, who was the main code breaker, worked out a pair of 'cribs' – words or phrases she predicted were likely to appear in a serial killer's message, and thus act as keys to unlocking the rest. Calculating the killer was egotistical and would seek attention for his crimes, Bettye guessed that the message would begin with the pronoun 'I'. It did. Bettye also postulated that the word 'kill' or even the phrase, 'I like killing' might appear. She was correct on all counts, and with these cribs, she and her husband were able to decipher almost the entire message. In plain text, it read:

> I like killing people because it is so much fun it is more fun than killing wild game in the forest because man is the most dangerous animal of all to kill something gives me the most thrilling experience it is even better than getting your rocks off with a girl the best part of it is that when I die I will be reborn in paradise and all the (people) I have killed will become my slaves I will not give you my name because you will try to slow down or stop my collecting of slaves for my afterlife.

The message ended with 18 symbols that to this day remain undeciphered. Some people believe these constitute an alternative code that may, when it is broken, reveal the Zodiac's name. Others think they are no more than random symbols included to make the code more difficult – or downright impossible – to break. The phrase 'the most dangerous animal of all' has been seen as a reference to a short story, 'The Most Dangerous Game' by Richard Connell. In this, a psychotic 'General Zaroff' (we note the same Z initial in the name) captured shipwrecked sailors, gave them a three-hour head start, then hunted them down and killed them unless they managed to outfox him.

On 4 August 1969, in response to a police request for proof that the writer of the Zodiac letters was genuinely the man who had actually committed the murders, the Zodiac sent a fourth letter to the *San Francisco Examiner*. Dubbed the 'Debut of Zodiac' letter, because the writer identifies himself by that name for the first time, it reads:

This is the Zodiac speaking. In answer to your asking for more details about the good times I have had in Vallejo, I shall be very happy to supply even more material. By the way, are the police having a good time with the code? If not, tell them to cheer up; when they do crack it, they will have me. On the 4th of July I did not open the car door. The window was rolled down all ready. The boy [Michael Mageau] was origionaly sitting in the front seat when I began fireing. When I fired the first shot at his head, he leaped backwards at the same time, thus spoiling my aim. He ended up on the back seat then the floor in back thrashing out very violently with his legs; that's how I shot him in the knee. I did not leave the cene of the killing with squealling tires + raceing engine as described in the Vallejo paper. I drove away quite slowly so as not to draw attention to my car. The man who told police that my car was brown was a negro about 40–45 rather shabbly dressed. I was in this phone booth having some fun with the Vallejo cop when he was walking by. When I hung the phone up the damn thing began to ring & that drew his attention to me + my car.

Last Christmass In that epasode the police were wondering how I could shoot + hit my victims in the dark. They did not openly state this, but implied this by saying it was a well lit night + I could see silowets on the horizon. Bullshit that area is srounded by high hills + trees. What I did was tape a small pencel flash light to the barrel of my gun. If you notice, in the center of the beam of light if you aim it at a wall or ceiling you will see a black or darck spot in the center of the circle of light about 3 to 6 inches across. When taped to a gun barrel, the bullet will strike in the center of the black dot in the light. All I had to do was spray them as if it was a water hose; there was no need to use the gun sights. I was not happy to see that I did not get front page coverage. [All spellings and grammar as original.]

The Zodiac made sure, among other things, to counter Blue Rock Springs Park caretaker's son George Bryant's claim that he had 'taken off at high speed burning rubber' when he left the scene. It was clever psychology by the police to set Zodiac the challenge. His quick response tended to confirm that the Zodiac killer was attention seeking, vain in the extreme and more than a little thin-skinned.

The Zodiac killer's MO was now largely set. But since his targets were apparently chosen at random, there was no way of predicting where he might next strike.

Late in the afternoon of 27 September 1969, college students Cecelia Ann Shepard (22), and Bryan Calvin Hartnell (20), were enjoying a sunny day together on the shores of Lake Berryessa, a recreation area 30 miles or so north of Napa, California. The water was blue and calm: the silence reassuring. They were lying on a picnic blanket, Cecelia's head on Bryan's lap as she read a book. Catching movement from the corner of her eye, Cecelia glanced up and noticed a man walking down the slope towards them. She went back to her book, but when she glanced up again, she saw that the stranger was watching them silently from the shadows of some nearby trees. Alarmed, she grabbed hold of Hartnell's arm and pointed. Realising he'd been spotted, the man stepped behind a tree.

A few seconds later, the man reappeared. 'Oh my God, he's got a gun!' Cecelia whispered. It wasn't the only horror. Now he had graduated to daylight attacks, the broadly built figure had put on a dark, executioner's-style hooded smock that reached to the waist. Cut with eye slits, the smock had a circular, white symbol emblazoned on the front. It looked like the crosshairs of a gun sight.

With the pistol in his hand trained steadily on the couple, the man strode up to them and stopped about ten feet away.

Through the eyeholes in the hood they saw that he had a fringe of brown hair. In a further attempt at disguise he was wearing a pair of clip-on sunglasses.

In a calculated effort to prevent any initial resistance, the man told them he was an escaped convict (possibly, although his speech was muffled by the hood, from Deer Lodge Prison, Montana). He said he'd killed a guard and stolen a vehicle. Pointing the pistol at Hartnell, he said, 'I want your money and your car keys. I have a stolen car, and I have nothing to lose. Then I can make it to Mexico.' Hartnell handed over the items. In the hopes of normalising the situation, he then tried to engage the stranger in conversation.

It didn't work. Producing some pre-cut lengths of plastic-coated washing line, the hooded man ordered Shepard to tie Hartnell's hands. In a whispered undertone, Bryan said, 'What about I go for his gun?'

'No,' Cecelia said, 'it might make things worse.' The stranger watched them intently through the eye slits. Cecelia tied Bryan up, but not tightly. Once he was satisfied that Hartnell was restrained, the stranger stepped back. Binding Cecelia's wrists in turn, he then retied Hartnell's hands, making sure they were tightly bound. He then made them both lie face down on the ground. Bryan asked, 'Is that gun really loaded?' Ejecting the magazine and turning the clip so that they could see the topmost bullet, the man said, 'Indeed it is.' But he didn't shoot.

Instead, in an act of deliberate and premeditated cruelty, he drew a knife. Then, without uttering a word, he began to stab them.

Hartnell suffered six knife wounds. In a desperate bid to survive he went still, controlled his breathing and feigned death. Shepard may have rolled around trying to escape. It's also possible that the attacker deliberately rolled her over. He stabbed her ten times – five in the back, and five in front.

Breaking off as soon as he was satisfied he'd murdered his victims, the killer walked away. Hartnell's ploy had worked – the attacker thought he was dead. Fighting against the pain, Bryan untied his own and Cecelia's bonds and began yelling. After what must have seemed to him an hour but was in fact a matter of minutes, a passing fisherman, Ronald Fong, heard the cries. He steered his boat into the shore and asked them if they needed help.

Before leaving the scene, the Zodiac had used a felt marker pen to draw the crosshairs symbol he now used as a macabre calling card on the door of Hartnell's Volkswagen Karmann Ghia. The message listed all three of the Zodiac's recent attacks. It ended with a chilling aide memoire of the latest: 'Sept 27-69-6:30 by knife.'

At about 7:40 p.m., a man called the Napa County Sheriff's department. 'I want to report a murder – no, a double murder,' he said. 'They are two miles north of park headquarters. They were in a white Volkswagen Karmann Ghia.' Officer David Slaight, who took the call, asked the man to provide his name and location. He replied, 'I'm the one who did it,' and hung up. The call was traced to a public phone booth at a car wash in Napa.

Cecelia Shepard died of her injuries before she could receive help.

The fact that the killer positively revelled in stabbing two innocent and harmless young people is hard to shake from the memory.

In the opinion of Dr D.E. Petris, the pathologist who performed the autopsy, the weapon used was 'from 9 to 11 inches in length and one inch in width, possibly sharpened on both sides . . . and similar to a bayonet type weapon. In addition, the wounds indicated it would be a heavy or sturdy type blade.' Investigators found size 10 footprints leading to and from the crime scene, made by the 'Wing Walkers' brand of boots. The Sheriff's office circulated sketches of the killer in the hooded costume, together with an artist's impression of a man seen in the area on the day of the attack.

No one was ever arrested for the crime.

The Zodiac killer's seventh and final confirmed victim did not fit the pattern established in the three previous attacks in any way.

On 11 October 1969, 29-year-old taxi driver Paul Stine arrived for work at the Yellow Cab Company, San Francisco, at approximately 8.45 p.m. His first job took him from Pier 68 to the San Francisco Air Terminal. About an hour later, between 9.30 and 9.45 p.m., he was tasked to pick up a fare at 500, 9th Avenue, and then drop off at Washington and Maple in the wealthy neighbourhood of Presidio Heights. Instead, at 9.55 p.m., the cab drew up a little way short of the Washington and Cherry Street intersection.

There, the passenger shot Stine in the right side of the head, killing him instantly. The killer then calmly stepped out of the cab, cut off a segment of the dead man's shirt, wiped down sections of the car to erase his own fingerprints and made off on foot.

By chance, three young teenagers had witnessed the murder from a house on the opposite side of Washington Street. In an emergency call made to the police and logged at 9.58 p.m., one of the young men described the suspect as 'A white male, 25–30 years old, 5'8" to 5'9", stocky build, reddish-brown hair worn in a crew cut, heavy rimmed glasses and dark clothing.' This description and the observations of the other two witnesses helped provide the only known police sketch of the killer.

The trio testified that the killer had bent over his victim for some time. (We now know that he was removing a large portion of the cab driver's shirt.) He then walked calmly to Cherry

Street, headed north onto Jackson Street and turned right and east towards the Jackson and Maple Street intersection. Driving through the crossroads, two police officers responding to the alert spotted a man answering the exact description the teenagers had given. But somehow, and for reasons that have never become entirely clear, the police dispatcher had told them to watch out for a 'black male suspect'. With this simple, terrible, and we have to hope not crudely racist mistake, the police missed the best chance they would ever have to catch the Zodiac killer.

The Zodiac had made good his escape. Why did he choose to kill a cab driver on this occasion, and not a courting couple? What had changed? What was the emotional payoff for him on this occasion, if any? One answer might be that he was enjoying his grotesque fame, and wanted more of it. The other possibility is that Paul Stine died for no other reason than a simple, every-day quibble over a cab fare.

Whatever the motive for this murder, with the repulsive arro-gance that had by now become only too familiar, the Zodiac was not slow to brag about it. In a letter to the *San Francisco Chronicle* postmarked 13 October 1969, the killer claimed responsibility for the Stine murder, enclosed a piece of the vic-tim's shirt to prove it, and mocked the San Francisco police for failing to catch him. He also threatened to 'wipe out a school bus some morning. Just shoot out the front tire + then pick off the kiddies as they come bouncing out.' In its entirety, the letter read:

This is the Zodiac speaking.
I am the murderer of the taxi driver over by Washington
St + Maple St last night, to prove this here is a blood
stained piece of his shirt. I am the same man who did in
the people in the north bay area.

The S.F. Police could have caught me last night if they
had searched the park properly instead of holding road
races with their motorcicles seeing who could make the
most noise. The car drivers should have just parked their
cars and sat there quietly waiting for me to come out of
cover.
School children make nice targets, I think I shall wipe out
a school bus some morning. Just shoot out the front tire
+ then pick off the kiddies as they come bouncing out.

Another letter, postmarked 8 November 1969, arrived at
the *Chronicle* office with a second piece of Paul Stine's shirt,
a taunting postcard depicting a pen washed in blood, and a
new, 340-symbol cipher – the 'Z 340'. Made up of 340 symbols whose meaning is not wholly understood, this cipher has
never been decoded, and continues to challenge code breakers
worldwide.

Many more letters followed, the majority addressed as before
to the *San Francisco Chronicle*. Postmarked 20 April 1970, the
letter with a new code, 'Z 13', contained a 13-symbol cipher
and a diagram of a bomb the Zodiac said would make good
on his threat to attack a school bus. In this letter, he claimed to
have killed ten people to date.

It was followed by a greetings card postmarked 28 April
1970. This demanded that the Zodiac killer's bus bomb
threats be made public, and that the people of the San Francisco Bay area wear 'Zodiac buttons' featuring the crosshairs
symbol.

When this didn't happen, he sent another letter, dated 26
June 1970, complaining about the public's failure to celebrate
his murderous activity. With it he enclosed what became known
as the 'Z 32' cipher. This included a map of the greater San
Francisco area signed with the crosshairs symbol marked at the

cardinal points with numbers. Near it was the message, 'is to be set to Mag N'. The note claimed: 'The map coupled with this code will tell you where the bomb is set. You have until next Fall to dig it up.'

A tireless self-publicist, the Zodiac sent many more messages and letters, including one, postmarked 1 August 1973, to the *Albany Union Times* newspaper in New York State. This one addressed rumours that he might have died or been hospitalised.

It read (the capital letters are accurate):

YOU ARE WRONG I'M NOT DEAD OR IN THE
HOSPITAL I AM ALIVE AND WELL AND IM
GOING TO START KILLING AGAIN Below is the
NAME AND LOCATION OF MY NEXT VICTIM
But you had Better hurry because I'm going to kill
Her August 10th at 5:00 P.M. when the shift change.
ALBANY is a nice town.'

This further threat led both federal and local police investigators to increase their efforts to catch the serial killer, and shift the focus of their inquiries to Albany, but once again, there were no arrests.

Theories

There are almost as many theories about the Zodiac killer as there are investigators to have them. Most are intriguing; many have merit; and all, if they help lead to the killer's identity, are in the public interest. The Internet is also alive with proposed solutions of the Zodiac ciphers. In a History Channel documentary, the renowned code-breaking expert Craig Bauer claimed to have solved the second encrypted message 'Z 340'. Part of his solution reads 'RICHERD'.*

The Zodiac disappeared from view around 1974. The main suspect at the time, Arthur Leigh Allen, was cleared by DNA evidence taken from saliva found on the envelope flaps of the killer's numerous letters to the media. Now, as DNA analysis becomes ever more effective, Vallejo Police Department detectives have sent the envelopes to a private laboratory for further testing. If the lab can find partial or whole DNA matches in the dried saliva, detectives can cross-match these against online genealogy databases, and so begin to build the killer's family tree. Then, gradually and by means of painstaking work, they may be able to home in on him.

This method was used recently to identify and arrest 72-year-old Joseph James DeAngelo for a raft of alleged crimes. Between 1975 and 1986 a serial killer, serial rapist and burglar known as the 'Golden State Killer' committed at least 12 murders, more than 50 rapes and over 100 burglaries. At the time of writing, Mr DeAngelo, a former law enforcement officer, remains in custody awaiting trial for the alleged offences.

The Twisted Legacy

The Zodiac myth machine has infiltrated popular culture right around the world, especially in the USA. The murders inspired the 'Scorpio' killer in the cult Clint Eastwood movie *Dirty Harry* (1971), as well as a flashback in the 2012 film *Seven Psychopaths*.

In three of his messages, the Zodiac – or a copycat – included references to Gilbert and Sullivan's comic opera *The Mikado*

---

* An interesting if sceptical discussion thread about that can be found here: http://scienceblogs.de/klausis-krypto-kolumne/2017/12/14/heres-the-solution-of-the-second-zodiac-cryptogram-or-maybe-not/

that would supposedly help reveal his name. They did not.

It is worth remembering that the killer was not glamorous, or dashing, or even especially clever. What he did was random, vile and entirely despicable. It was only the random nature of the attacks that helped him escape, and an unfortunate mistake that prevented his arrest. The truth? The so-called 'Zodiac' was a pathetic coward who surprised his victims before they had a chance to defend themselves, and then, in the case of Shepard and Hartnell, attacked them with cold-hearted, premeditated cruelty.

Despite a 45-year hunt conducted by amateur and professional sleuths alike, the Zodiac killer has never been brought to justice. He may still be alive.

Fenn's Treasure

'A treasure of incalculable value...gold of antique date and of great variety...diamonds – some of them exceedingly large and fine – a hundred and ten in all, and not one of them small; eighteen rubies of remarkable brilliancy; three hundred and ten emeralds, all very beautiful; and twenty-one sapphires, with an opal.'

The Gold Bug, by Edgar Allan Poe

Why has no one been able to find an ancient bronze chest filled with fabulous treasures worth more than one million dollars, and hidden somewhere in one of four US states? In his 2010 book *The Thrill of the Chase*, ex-US military pilot and Vietnam War veteran Forrest Fenn published a poem and some hints that give clues to the treasure's location. Mr Fenn says the hoard includes: 'two Ceylon sapphires, hundreds of rubies, eight emeralds and lots of diamonds'. Which is very like Poe's imaginary treasure, but has the great advantage of being real, and lies ready to enrich the person or persons who are smart enough to find it. The chest also contains dozens of solid gold nuggets, two of which weigh more than one troy pound apiece; a strand of Mayan gold beads; a number of pre-Columbian gold figures between 1,500 and 1,800 years old; a silver bracelet studded with turquoise of historical significance that Mr Fenn would like to buy back from the finder; a jar of Alaskan gold dust; and no fewer than 265 gold coins, mostly American Eagles and Double Eagles. A treasure trove worth finding, then – just a bit.

In the eight years since the treasure was hidden, more than 100,000 people have gone out into the wilds of New Mexico, Colorado, Wyoming and Montana armed with their own personal solutions to the puzzle, buoyed with the headiest cocktail of all: hope. So far, no one has found it – although Fenn believes that a couple of people may have come within 200 feet of the cache. How does he know this? We don't know. One thing is for certain: Mr Fenn has achieved one of his main aims in creating the treasure hunt, which was to 'get people off the couch and into the wilderness . . . I wanted to get people interested, energized and outside.'

Here is the poem from the book:

As I have gone alone in there
And with my treasures bold,
I can keep my secret where,
And hint of riches new and old.

Begin it where warm waters halt
And take it in the canyon down,
Not far, but too far to walk.
Put in below the home of Brown.

From there it's no place for the meek,
The end is ever drawing nigh;
There'll be no paddle up your creek,
Just heavy loads and water high.

If you've been wise and found the blaze,
Look quickly down, your quest to cease,
But tarry scant with marvel gaze,

Just take the chest and go in peace.

So why is it that I must go
And leave my trove for all to seek?
The answers I already know,
I've done it tired, and now I'm weak.

So hear me all and listen good,
Your effort will be worth the cold.
If you are brave and in the wood
I give you title to the gold.

According to the map, the treasure is in one of four states: Montana, Wyoming, Colorado or New Mexico. Many believe it is in New Mexico, which, while it narrows down the search area by a huge factor, still leaves a lot of very wild and sometimes dangerous ground to cover.

Fenn says there are subtle extra hints in his related books 'if you know how to recognize them'. He has also given out a number of extra clues since first publication, many of them common sense and straightforward:

You should start with the first clue and follow the others con-secutively to the treasure. The most common mistake that I see searchers make is that they underestimate the importance of the first clue. If you don't have that one nailed down, you might as well stay home and play Canasta. Although many have tried, I doubt that anyone will find the blaze before they have figured out the first clue. Read my book in a normal manner. Then read the poem over and over and over, slowly – thinking. Then read my book again, this time looking for subtle hints that will help solve the clues.

The clues are consecutive. Excellent research materials to

decipher the Poem are the book, Google Earth and/or a good map.

There are a few words in the poem that are not useful in finding the treasure, but it is risky to discount any of them. You oversimplify the clues. There are many places in the Rocky Mountains where warm waters halt, and nearly all of them are north of Santa Fe. Look at the big picture; there are no short cuts.

There isn't a human trail in very close proximity to where I hid the treasure. Please don't overextend yourself. I was 80 or about when I hid the treasure and it was not a difficult task. You don't have to move big rocks, or scale a precipice to get to the treasure. Stay away from dangerous terrain. I made two trips from my car to the hiding place and it was done in one afternoon.

Read the clues in my poem over and over and study maps of the Rocky Mountains. Try to marry the two. The treasure is out there waiting for the person who can make all the lines cross in the right spot.

If your solve is in the desert, get a new solve, and remember, much of the Rio Grande River is not in the Rocky Mountains.

The treasure is located above 5,000 ft. and below 10,200 ft. It is at least 8.25 miles north of Santa Fe, New Mexico. [These sets of figures are both oddly precise – why?]

If you knew the geographic location of each clue it would be a map to the treasure.

It is not in an outhouse, a graveyard, a mine, a tunnel or a cave – and it is not under a man-made object or associated with any structure.

It is not in a dangerous place and can be retrieved in one afternoon if you know where to go. It is not necessary to move any large rocks or climb up a steep precipice. If you think I could not have put it there, you are probably right.

'Where warm waters halt' does not refer to a dam.

A few of the extra clues are more gnomic:

I think kids have an advantage [when it comes to finding the treasure]. Don't ask me to explain that.

That poem was really written by an architect. Every word was placed in there strategically, and you can't ignore any of the nouns.

Many are giving serious thought to the clues in my poem, but only a few are in tight focus with a word that is key.

My church is in the mountains and along the river bottoms where dreams and fantasies alike go to play.

The treasure chest is wet. [Does this mean it is beneath and/ or behind a waterfall?]

Rocking chair ideas can lead one to the first few clues, but a physical presence is needed to complete the solve. Google Earth cannot help with the last clue.

Mr Fenn's life story is almost as intriguing as the puzzle he set. He joined the US Air Force in 1950, training initially as a radar mechanic and reaching the rank of Sergeant. Three years later, he entered pilot training, and upon completion was commissioned as a Second Lieutenant. Fenn served with American forces in Germany flying the F100C and F 'Super Sabre' fighters, before being posted to Vietnam in January 1968. And right into the hottest part of a very hot war. Promoted Major, he commanded the airbase at Tuy Hoa, flying no fewer than 328 combat missions. He was shot down twice, but survived and eluded capture on both occasions. The first time, he 'dead-sticked' an F100D when its engines failed, managing to stop the aircraft on the ground in the very short space of 340 feet. The second time, he was shot down over Laos by a North Vietnamese Army

ZSU anti-aircraft gun. He ejected over Tchepone, hiding out in the jungle before 'The Candy Ann', one of the USAF's fleet of 'Jolly Green Giant' Sikorsky HH-3E combat search and rescue helicopters, picked him up the next day.

Quitting the Air Force in 1970, Fenn packed his family into the car at the suggestion of his wife, Peggy, and moved to northern New Mexico. Picking up on a boyhood love for ancient artefacts, he opened an art foundry and gallery in Santa Fe. The picturesque town is, he comments laconically, 'the only place I knew where I could wear Hush Puppies and blue jeans and make a living'. Make one he certainly did. He sold the business after 17 years, and then wrote '11 books on art, archaeology, history, ethnology, a few biographies and three memoirs'.

It may be that by the time this book is published, or some time during its life cycle, Fenn's treasure will be found. But Mr Fenn makes some intriguing comments about its genesis: 'I see my memoir as being a story that was ordained by some unknown hand. It came to me at age eighty as though my entire life had been waiting for that moment. The bulk of the book was written in six weeks, and phrases that I had never thought of before suddenly appeared on my computer screen . . .'

Now that's mysterious.

Picture Credits

The author and publisher are grateful to Getty Images for permission to reproduce the illustrations on pp. 1, 2, 4 (above), 5, 6, 10, 11; and to Alamy for pp. 2, 3, 4 (below), 7, 8, 9.

Bibliography and Sources

The Shugborough Code

1. *An Authentic Journal of the late Expedition under Commodore George Anson*
Author: Midshipman John Philips
Publisher: original edition: J. Robinson, at the Golden Lion in Ludgate Street, London, 1744
Facsimile edition: Gale Sabin Americana, 2009

2. Author's interviews with National Trust staff at Shugborough Hall

3. *Log of the* Centurion *Based on the Original Papers of Captain Philip Saumarez on Board HMS* Centurion, *Lord Anson's Flagship During His Circumnavigation, 1740–44*
Author: Leo Heaps/Philip Saumarez
Publisher: New York, Macmillan Publishing Co., Inc., (1974)

Atlantis

1. *Timaeus and Critias*
Author: Plato
Publisher: Penguin Classics, 2008

2. *Atlantis: The Antediluvian World*
Author: Ignatius L. Donnelly
Publisher: HarperCollins 1981

3. *The Agricola and the Germania*
Author: Tacitus
Publisher: Penguin Books, 2000

4. 'Lost City of Atlantis "buried in Spanish wetlands"'

Article by Edward Owen, *Daily Telegraph*, 14 March 2011

5. *The Path of the Pole*
Author: Charles H. Hapgood
Publisher: Souvenir Press Ltd, 2001

6. *Maps of the Ancient Sea Kings*
Author: Charles H. Hapgood
Publisher: Souvenir Press Ltd, 2001

7. *Excavations at Thera, Volumes I-VII*
Author: Spyridon Marinatos
Publisher: Vivlioth, 1968

8. *Finding Atlantis*
National Geographic TV documentary, 2016

9. *Atlantis Rising*
National Geographic TV documentary, 2016

The Mary Celeste

1. *The Story of the Mary Celeste*
Author: Charles Edey Fay
Edition: illustrated reprint
Publisher: Dover Publications, 1988

2. 'J. Hzabakuk Jesphson's Statement'
Author: Sir Arthur Conan Doyle
Publisher: Cornhill Magazine, 1844

3. Wikipedia: https://en.wikipedia.org/wiki/Mary_Celeste

4. Prof. Andrea Sella, UCL. Personal telephone interview and email exchanges, permission granted to name him and report the experiment

5. *New York Herald*, 15 March 1873, p.8

Göbekli Tepe

1. http://gobeklitepe.info

2. *The Garden of Eden: Revealed*
Television documentary by Blink Entertainment Ltd, 2017
For Channel 5 (UK) and the Smithsonian Channel in association with
France 5, SBS, TV Australia and BBC Worldwide

The Great Pyramid of Giza

1. *The History of Architecture*
Author: Gaynor Aaltonen
Publisher: Arcturus, 2008
Gaynor Aaltonen's research notes

2. *The Great Pyramid – Treasures Decoded*
Television documentary by Blink Entertainment Ltd, 2014
For Channel 4 (UK) and the Smithsonian Channel in association
with France 5, SBS, Shaw Media, Historia, TV Australia and BBC
Worldwide

3. *The Great Pyramid – The New Evidence*
Television documentary by Windfall Films/Alibi Entertainment in
association with CBC Canada, Fronace TV & Science Channel, 2017

Stonehenge

1. *The History of Architecture*
Author: Gaynor Aaltonen
Publisher: Arcturus, 2008
Gaynor Aaltonen's research notes

2. *Craig Rhos-y-felin: a Welsh Bluestone Megalith Quarry for
Stonehenge*
Authors: Mike Parker Pearson, Richard Bevins, Rob Ixer, Joshua
Pollard
Publisher and Copyright: Antiquity Publications Ltd, 2016
https://doi.org/10.15184/aqy.2015.177

3. *Operation Stonehenge: What Lies Beneath*
BBC 2 TV documentary, 2014, two episodes

4. Salisbury Museum, Wiltshire: standing exhibitions, inc. Amesbury Archer

Teotihuacan

1. *The History of Architecture*
Author: Gaynor Aaltonen
Publisher: Arcturus, 2008
Gaynor Aaltonen's research notes

2. 'Lakes of mercury and human sacrifices – after 1,800 years, Teotihuacan reveals its treasures'
Guardian – Paul Laity, 24 Sep 2017

The Nasca Lines

1. *The Lines and Geoglyphs of Nasca and Palpa*
UNESCO World Heritage Centre website:
http://whc.unesco.org/en/list/700#links

Easter Island

1. *Easter Island – Archaeology, Ecology and Culture*
Author: Jo Anne Van Tilburg
Publisher: British Museum Press, 1994

2. *Easter Island – Mysteries of a Lost World*
Television documentary by zodiak media/iwc media/BBC, 2013
Written & directed by Jago Cooper
Photographed, produced & directed by Spike Geilinger

The Loch Ness Monster

1. *Marise*
Author: Stephen Lister

Publisher: Peter Davies, London, 1950

2. *The Enigma of Loch Ness: Making Sense of a Mystery*
Author: H. H. Bauer
Publisher: Urbana and Chicago: Univ. of Illinois Press, 1968

3. *Daily Mail*, 21 April 1934

4. *Sunday Telegraph* – 'Mandrake', 7 December 1975

5. *More Than a Legend*
Author: Constance Whyte
Publisher: Hamish Hamilton, London, 1957, & ibid third impression 1961.

6. *Life of St Columba*
Author: Adomnán
Publisher: Penguin Books Ltd, 1995
Translator: Richard Sharpe

7. *Itinerarium Scotiae (The Journey Through Scotland)*
Author: Walter of Bingham
Retrieved 2018 from:
http://blogs.bl.uk/digitisedmanuscripts/2013/03/loch-ness-monster-found-at-british-library.html

8. *A Monstrous Commotion: The Mysteries of Loch Ness*
Author: Gareth Williams
Publisher: Orion Books Ltd, London 2015

9. 'Researchers Hunting for Environmental DNA in Loch Ness'
Article 2 July 2018 by News Staff/Source
Publisher: Sci-News.com website

Bigfoot and Other Suspects

1. *On the Track of Bigfoot*
Author: Marian T. Place
Publisher: Dodd, Mead & Company, 1974

2. *Bigfoot: The Life and Times of a Legend*

Author: Joshua Blu Buhs
Publisher: The University of Chicago Press, 2009

3. The Bigfoot Field Researchers Organisation website:
https://www.bfro.net

The Green Children of Woolpit

1. *Historia rerum Anglicarum*
Author: William of Newburgh
Publisher: Internet Ancient History Sourcebook, Fordham University

2. *Chronicon Anglicanum*
Author: Ralph of Coggeshall (orig. Latin & French texts)
Publisher: Cambridge University Press, 2012

3. *The Midwich Cuckoos*
Author: John Wyndham
Publisher: Ballantine Books, 1958

The Phaistos Disc

1. *The History of Architecture*
Author: Gaynor Aaltonen
Publisher: Arcturus, 2008

2. And Gaynor Aaltonen's research notes/interview with Spyridon
Marinatos

The Cat in the Box

1. *Albert Einstein, Philosopher-Scientist: The Library of Living Philosophers, Vol. VII, 7*
Editor: Paul Arthur Schlipp
Publisher: Open Court Publishing, 1949

2. *'Die gegenwärtige Situation in der Quantenmechanik'* ('The present situation in quantum mechanics')
Author: Erwin Schrödinger
Quoted in *Naturwissenchaften*, Nov. 1935, 23 (48) pp. 807-812

Publisher: Springer Science + Business Media

The Wow! Signal

1.*The Big Ear Wow! Signal: What We Know and Don't Know About It After 20 Years*
Author: Dr Jerry R. Ehman
Original Draft completed: 1 September 1997
Last Revision: 3 February 1998. Copyright © 1997-2008 Big Ear Radio Observatory and North American AstroPhysical Observatory

2. 'Fast Radio Bursts' – *Nature*, 7 January 2019
https://www.nature.com/articles/d41586-019-00049-5

The Rising Star Cave

1. *Homo naledi*, a new species of the genus *Homo* from the Dinaledi Chamber, South Africa
Authors: Lee R. Berger, John Hawks, Darryl J. Ruiter et al
Publisher: elife magazine, 10 September 2015.
https://elifesciences.org/articles/09560?page=3

2. http://www.nhm.ac.uk/discover/homo-naledi-your-most-recently-discovered-human-relative.html (Material cited in this article features in the book, *Our Human Story*, by Dr Louise Humphrey and Prof. Chris Stringer)

Area 51

1. *Roswell Daily Record*, 9 July 1947: 'Harrassed Rancher who Located "Saucer" Sorry He Told About it', and other dates, ibid

2. *Secret History: Conspiracies from Ancient Aliens to the New World Order*
Author: Nick Redfern
Publisher: Visible Ink Press, 2015

3. *Roswell in Perspective*
Author: Karl Pflock

Publisher: Fund for UFO Research, 1994

4. *Beyond Roswell: Alien Autopsy Film, Area 51 and the US Government Coverup of UFOs*
Authors: Michael Hesemann and Philip Mantle
Publisher: Da Capo Press, 1997

5. *Crash at Corona*
Authors: Stanton T. Friedman and Don Berliner
Publisher: Paragon House, 1992

6. Mutual UFO Network [MUFON] internet site: https://www.mufon.com/roswell-ufo-retrieval---1947.html

7. Ray Santill footage in documentary entitled: Alien Autopsy: Fact or Fiction? broadcast on Fox television 28 August 1995 (available on IMDB)

8. *Eamonn Investigates: Alien Autopsy* (British Sky Broadcasting, April 2006)

9. Alien Autopsy: The True Story (British Sky Broadcasting, 2006)

10. 'Glowing Auras and Black Money': The Pentagon's Mysterious UFO Program', *New York Times*, 16 December 2017

11. *The Rough Guide to Conspiracy Theories*
Authors: James McConnachie, Robin Tudge
Publisher: Rough Guides Ltd, 2005

The Zodiac Killer

1. http://www.zodiackiller.com website: *Letters & other material* by kind permission of Tom Voigt

2. https://www.zodicciphers.com website - archive retrieved various dates

Fenn's Treasure

1. *The Thrill of the Chase*
Author: Forrest Fenn
Publisher: One Horse Land & Cattle Limited Company, 2010

Index